Travel and Tourism for Vocational A Level

Teacher Support Pack

Lindsey Taylor
Tony Outhart
Ray Barker
Alan Marvell

Published by HarperCollins*Publishers* Limited
77–85 Fulham Palace Road
Hammersmith
London
W6 8JB

www.**Collins**Education.com
On-line support for schools and colleges

First published 2001

ISBN 0 00 711385 4

Lindsey Taylor, Tony Outhart, Ray Barker and Alan Marvell assert the moral right to be identified as the authors of this work.

British Cataloguing in Publication Data.
A cataloguing record for this publication is available from the British Library.

Commissioned by Kay Wright
Series designed by DSM Partnership
Cover designed by Patricia Briggs
Cover picture by Tony Stone
Project managed, edited and typeset by DSM Partnership
Illustrations by Barking Dog Art
Production by James Graves
Printed and bound by Martin's The Printers Ltd, Berwick-upon-Tweed

Contents

Purpose and structure of the teacher support pack

Vocational A levels were introduced in September 2000 to replace the existing Advanced GNVQs. They are designed to provide a broad-based education that will enable students to pursue further training, additional further education or higher education. Students' studies will allow them to develop a range of knowledge, understanding and skills within a specific vocational context. The old Advanced GNVQ in Leisure and Tourism has been replaced by two separate qualifications:

- the Vocational A level in Travel and Tourism
- the Vocational A level in Leisure and Recreation.

This teacher support pack has been designed to work alongside the Collins Educational textbook *Travel and Tourism for Vocational A Level.* A companion textbook and teacher pack supports the delivery of the Vocational A level in Leisure and Recreation.

The pack is designed to ensure that tutors can deliver the contents of the textbook easily and effectively. In essence, this support pack should take the hard work out of translating the textbook into coherent and stimulating lessons and activities. All textbook pages and activities are clearly listed throughout the resource pack to allow instant reference to relevant information.

Resources and delivery

The detailed plans in this pack suggest resources that might be used in delivering the award, and individual session plans explain how these might be used. As a general guide, students will need a wide range of brochures, leaflets and information from travel and tourism organisations for all units. These will also be needed to undertake some of the textbook's activities. Tutors might orchestrate the collection of materials by setting an induction activity in which students are required to collect information. A suitable resources storage area should be available. Students will also need access to the internet and a range of textbooks.

There is an excellent range of educational videos focusing on the travel and tourism industry; however, you can also make use of many mainstream television programmes such as consumer and travel shows. Fly-on-the-wall documentaries can provide a stimulating basis for group discussions.

Organised group visits and guest speakers should form an important part of the delivery of the qualification. These allow students to identify and evaluate key travel and tourism issues first hand.

There is a wide range of teaching and delivery strategies that will be appropriate for the Vocational A level. Group discussions, brainstorming, problem solving, case studies, role play and research activities are all useful ways of increasing students' understanding of the industry, as well as helping to develop key skills and evaluation skills.

Unit session plans

The core of this pack consists of detailed session plans for each of the six compulsory units of the full award:

- Unit 1 – Investigating travel and tourism
- Unit 2 – Tourism development
- Unit 3 – Worldwide travel destinations
- Unit 4 – Marketing in travel and tourism
- Unit 5 – Customer service in travel and tourism
- Unit 6 – Travel and tourism in action.

Each unit is presented in 15 session plans. Tutors may find it useful to use these plans as the basis for a scheme of work and individual lesson plans. Where units are delivered over the whole academic year, each session plan would provide lessons for two consecutive weeks (providing a 30-week programme). Additional weeks during the academic year may be used for organised group visits or work placements.

Each section contains an introduction. This covers the nature of the unit content, highlighting what is important in teaching and learning terms. Suggestions are provided on delivery and the resources needed to teach the unit. The introduction also outlines the links to the other five compulsory units so that tutors can combine learning points and activities where appropriate. Finally, there is a unit planner, providing a session-by-session overview of the content referenced to the textbook page numbers.

Session plans

These all have a series of common elements.

Session number

It is strongly recommended that sessions be delivered in numerical order since this reflects both the textbook and the Vocational A level specification sequence.

Textbook pages

Indicates the pages of the textbook that relate to the session. This can be used to clarify information that may be used in the session. In addition, you may like to refer students to the relevant pages in the book so that they can recap on the session through further reading.

Resources required

This gives guidance on any resources that may be beneficial to the session such as brochures, maps, etc. It also lists which, if any, of the photocopy masters provided in this pack can be used to support the teaching and delivery of the session.

Objectives of session

This provides a brief summary of the key topics that will be covered and may be used by tutors to introduce each session.

Development of textbook

Provides suggestions on how to deliver the key topics and information to be covered in the session. There are recommendations for effective group and individual learning activities based on the contents of the textbook. Any use of the relevant photocopy masters or handout is indicated.

Key words to define

This provides a list of key words and phrases introduced or covered in the session. You might like to use this list as a consolidation exercise to check students' learning and understanding of the key topics.

Answers to textbook activities

Each activity is referenced to the relevant textbook page number. This section provides suggested answers and/or recommendations as to how the activities could be used. There may be suggestions on how activities can be expanded to allow for greater depth and understanding.

Build your learning

This offers guidance on how to build on the content of the session by suggesting further activities or discussion points that students may find useful. Frequently, this contains suggestions for additional investigations that students could undertake outside the classroom, which may help them to produce the necessary assessment evidence.

Photocopy masters

Following the session plans for each unit, there are photocopy masters that can be used to support classroom delivery.

Assessment

Each unit has one assessment, which is outlined in the assessment evidence section of the unit specification. Units are assessed either through a portfolio of evidence or by an external assessment. Advice on preparing students for assessment is given in the session plans, and the final session or sessions are often structured to support this process in addition to consolidating learning.

External assessment

The form of external assessment varies between the three awarding bodies. However, the old Advanced GNVQ format of short multiple-choice papers is no longer used. External assessment for the Vocational A level in Travel and Tourism typically includes short-answer papers, which are frequently based on scenarios or pre-seen case study materials. Students need to develop and practice skills in tackling case studies before the external assessment. You might use sample external assessments from the awarding body together with case studies from the textbook to develop students' skills. If pre-seen materials are provided for an external assessment, you will need to ensure that sufficient curriculum time has been allocated to allow students to prepare for the assessment.

Internal assessment

Tutors might split the assessment into distinct tasks to allow students to gather evidence for their portfolios as the unit progresses rather than tackling the entire assessment on completion of the unit. You should meet regularly with individual students to discuss their progress and help them plan their work. All three awarding bodies provide pro formas for assessment sheets and portfolio index sheets.

Developing work-relatedness

The final section of the pack looks at the ways in which tutors can develop and organise vocationally relevant work experience for students. The section includes pro formas that can be used in the effective identification and management of work placements.

Unit session plans and photocopy masters

Unit 1: Investigating travel and tourism

Introduction

This unit aims to provide students with an overview of the structure and scale of the UK travel and tourism industry and introduces the wide range of products and services that are provided by travel and tourism organisations. Given the broad scope of the industry, you should not attempt to cover the scale and structure in great depth in this introductory unit. Work should concentrate on giving students an overview of the industry, highlighting where to find further information as necessary.

Delivery suggestions

This is an important unit since it lays the foundation for the study of many other units of the Vocational A level in Travel and Tourism. It is recommended that it is delivered at the beginning of the course. However, you may find it possible to deliver the final parts of the unit that cover working in the travel and tourism industry (pages 72–93 in the textbook) towards the end of course when students are thinking about moving on.

Organised visits and guest speakers will enhance students' understanding of the industry. Many of the activities in the textbook can be based on information drawn from the students' own locality or past travel experiences. Students should be encouraged to draw on their own experiences as customers and employees of travel and tourism organisations whenever possible.

Links to other units

Because this is an introductory unit, it links into all the other compulsory units. There are also links with all of the optional units.

Unit planner

Session	Session objectives	Text pages
1	To introduce the unit To define travel and tourism and other key industry terms and discuss the main types of tourism	4 to 7
2	To identify and discuss the reasons for the postwar development of the UK travel and tourism industry, covering: (a) changing socioeconomic conditions and (b) developing technology	8 to 17
3	To recap on previous session To identify and discuss reasons for the postwar development of the UK travel and tourism industry, covering: (c) product development and innovation and (d) changing consumer needs, expectations and fashions	18 to 28
4	To identify and discuss the key features of the travel and tourism industry, covering: (a) private sector, (b) public sector, (c) voluntary sector and (d) use of new technology	29 to 33
5	To recap on previous session To identify and discuss the key features of the travel and tourism industry, covering: (e) external pressures and (f) impact on host communities	33 to 38
6	To investigate the structure of the UK travel and tourism industry and to provide an overview of the six key industry components To review the supply structure and chain of distribution To investigate: (a) travel agencies	39 to 44
7	To investigate: (b) tour operations	44 to 53
8	To investigate: (c) transport and (d) accommodation and catering	53 to 58
9	To investigate: (e) tourism development and (f) tourist attractions To recap on previous sessions about the six components	58 to 66
10	To identify and discuss the scale and significance of the UK travel and tourism industry in terms of: (a) consumer spending and contribution to the balance of payments, (b) numbers employed nationally, (c) number of tourists coming into the UK and (d) number of domestic and outgoing tourists	67 to 71
11	To identify and discuss the range of employment opportunities in travel and tourism To identify the type of personal and technical skills required by employers	72 to 79
12	To investigate sources of information about jobs in travel and tourism To identify jobs that match students' interests, skills, qualifications and aspirations	79 to 85
13	To provide practical tips and advice on how to apply for jobs, covering letters of application, application forms and interview skills	86 to 93
14	To provide guidance on what to include in, and how to present, a CV	90 to 93
15	To consolidate the learning from the previous 14 sessions To discuss and coordinate the assessment evidence for the unit	452 to 453

Session 1

Textbook pages 4 to 7

Resources required

- Handout of unit specification
- Awarding body glossary of key terms
- Handout of key industry definitions from page 5 of the textbook (Figure 1.1)

Objectives of session

- To introduce the unit.
- To define travel and tourism and other key industry terms.
- To discuss the main types of tourism.

Development of textbook

- This session might be introduced by giving students a brief summary of what the unit will cover and what students will have to do to pass it. This information could be provided as a handout.
- Students need to understand the terms travel and tourism, the different categories of tourist and other key industry definitions. Use the definitions provided on pages 4 to 6 of the text as a starting point. Other key definitions could also be provided at this stage, such as product, goods, service, facility, event, customer and provider. These may also be defined in a glossary of key terms provided by your awarding body.
- Students should be able to identify the main categories of tourist (see activity on page 5) and the main reasons why people travel (see Figure 1.2).
- This session could involve a group quiz or question and answer session to confirm students' understanding of the key industry terms.

Key words to define

Tourism, leisure travel, business travel, tourist, day visitor, travel, domestic tourism, inbound tourism, outbound tourism, incoming tourist, outbound tourist, domestic tourist, long holiday, short-break holiday, short haul, long haul, inclusive tours/package holidays, all-inclusive holidays, independent holidays, seat only and fly-drive holidays.

Answers to textbook activities

Page 4: Key phrases in a definition of tourism might include: short-term movement of people; destinations away from where they live and work; activities during the trip, such as travel, day visits, eating, etc.

Page 5: Joan Dumas – business, day visitor, incoming; Jack Brooks – leisure, day visitor, domestic; The Jones' – leisure, tourist, outgoing; Batholomew Tapp – leisure, tourist, incoming.

Build your learning

The end of section activity on page 7 can be used to reinforce students' understanding of the key terms and definitions. You could also briefly introduce the six key industry components at this stage to provide students with an overview of the travel and tourism industry.

Session 2

Textbook pages 8 to 17

Resources required

- OHT 1
- Handout of Figure 1.3, key milestones chart
- Case study on pages 11 and 12
- Travel brochures and cross-Channel timetables

Access to the internet would also be useful for the activity on page 16. Relevant data about socioeconomic conditions is also available from *Social Trends, Annual Abstract of Statistics* and the internet *www.ons.gov.uk*, *www.statistics.gov.uk*, and *www.keynote.co.uk*.

Objectives of session

To identify and discuss the main reasons for the postwar development of the UK travel and tourism industry, covering:

(a) changing socioeconomic conditions
(b) developing technology.

Development of textbook

- OHT 1 can be used to introduce the four key interrelated factors that have led to the growth of the industry since the Second World War. This session looks at two of these factors.
- Figures 1.3 and 1.4 on pages 8 and 9 can be used to highlight key milestones in the development of the industry and trends in the number of holidays taken since 1951.
- Define the term socioeconomic and explain that these factors are all interrelated. Students should be aware that there have been significant increases in the amount of time available for leisure activities, including tourism. This is due largely to demographic and employment trends, such as shifts in population age structure, an increase in part-time workers, more people taking early retirement, increases in paid holiday entitlement, etc.
- Students need to understand the terms disposable income and household disposable income, and the impact of increasing disposable income on the travel and tourism industry. The case study on pages 11 and 12 can be used to illustrate how national economics affects travel and tourism.
- Students also need to understand how improvements in transport networks and personal mobility have increased demand for travel and tourism products and services. Use Figure 1.5 to highlight trends in car ownership in the UK. This could be expanded upon by discussing the impact of improved mobility on a selection of tourism facilities such as hotels, theatres, national parks, theme parks, etc.
- Developing technology has had a significant impact on the industry. The textbook provides two examples to illustrate the impact of transport technology: the introduction of jet aircraft leading to the growth of overseas package holidays (see Thomson case study, page 14); the impact of the Channel tunnel, fast sea catamarans and budget airlines on cross-Channel travel (see case study on page 15 and activity on page 16).
- Students also need to be aware of the impact of communications technology on the industry. Computer reservation systems (CRS) and global distribution systems (GDS) have revolutionised the way in which the industry operates. The internet now also provides consumers with options to deal direct with providers. If you have access to the internet, you could show students some well-known travel and tourism websites such as www.lastminute.com and www.easyjet.co.uk.

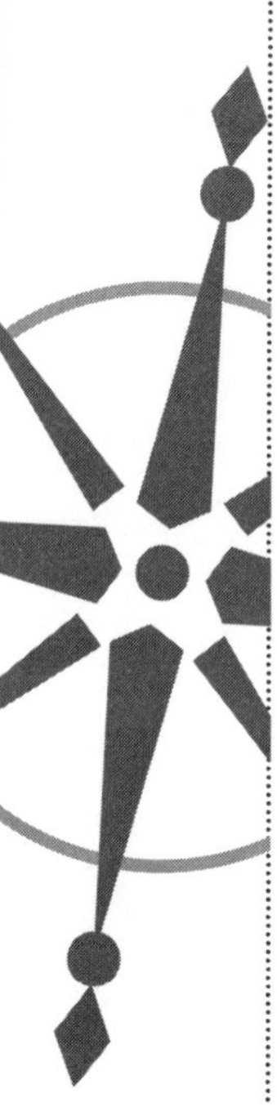

Key words to define

Socioeconomic, paid holiday entitlement, disposable income, computer reservation systems (CRS), global distribution systems (GDS).

Answers to textbook activities

Page 12: Main economic factors: general state of the economy, disposable income levels, impact of building society windfall payments, fear of unemployment during recession periods, proportion of population that are early retired, bank interest and mortgage rates, basic salary levels, availability of student grants, currency exchange rates, inflation.

Page 16: You will need to provide students with cross-Channel travel brochures, timetables and price lists to complete this activity. You may also find it useful to access the internet, particularly for details about budget 'no frills' airlines such as easyJet, Go and Ryanair.

Build your learning

Reinforce message that all these factors are interrelated and identify the two factors – product development and changing consumer needs, expectations and fashions – that will be covered in the next session.

Session 3

Textbook pages 18 to 28

Resources required

- OHT 1
- Top twentieth century travel innovations case study (pages 18 to 19)
- UK holiday centre and Butlin's case studies (pages 20 to 21)
- Handout of the A–Z of special interest holidays (Figure 1.7)
- Selection of tour operator brochures, including long-haul destinations, all-inclusives and UK holiday centres

Objectives of session

- To recap on previous session.
- To identify and discuss the main reasons for the postwar development of the UK travel and tourism industry, covering:
  (c) product development and innovation
  (d) changing consumer needs, expectations and fashions.

Development of textbook

- Use OHT 1 to recap from previous session and remind students that all the four key factors identified are interrelated.
- Students need to be aware that the travel industry is continually developing new, innovative products to meet consumer demand. You can use the case study on pages 18 and 19 to provide examples of three major twentieth century travel innovations. This can be developed by asking students what they think could be the major innovations of the twenty-first century (see activity on page 18).
- There are many examples, such as the promotion of the weekend break or short break, to illustrate how the domestic tourism industry has developed new products. You can use the case studies about UK holiday centres and Butlin's rebranding to show an example of new product development.
- You might find it useful to provide students with Figure 1.7, showing ABTA's A–Z list of special interest holiday categories, in order to illustrate the diversity of the travel industry. Other examples of successful product innovation include development of long-haul holidays, fly-drives, fly-cruises and all-inclusive tours.
- When discussing changing consumer needs, expectations and fashions it might be useful to use some local examples of tourism facilities that have experienced changes in popularity, such as nightclubs, bars, pubs, restaurants, cinemas, hotels, etc. The case studies on pages 20 and 21 and the activity on page 22 illustrate the impact of changing fashions on UK holiday centres. You can also use the press articles on pages 26 and 27 to provide further examples.

Key words to define

Changing consumer needs and expectations, changing fashions, innovative travel products, short-break.

Answers to textbook activities

Page 22 'Holiday centres': Most of the answers to the first task are contained in the case studies on pages 20 and 21. The holiday camp concept became popular in the 1950s and 1960s because entrepreneurs like Billy Butlin and Fred Pontin recognised that there would be great demand for families to take holidays in the immediate postwar years. They also successfully combined accommodation and catering with a full programme of entertainment that would appeal to whole families. By the 1980s the holiday camp concept

had become unfashionable because consumer needs and expectations had moved on. In many cases, the camp facilities had become dated due to lack of investment and the number of visitors fell dramatically. The camps were struggling to compete with foreign package holidays to countries like Spain, Greece and Italy. For task 3, it may be useful to provide students with recent brochures for a selection of holiday centres such as Butlin's, Center Parcs and Oasis. From these, they can identify examples of product development.

Page 22 'Special interest holiday categories': Students will need to access holiday brochures to complete task one. Some activities from the special interest holiday list that may cease to be provided include carpet weaving, Concorde experience, millennium, bungee jumping and hockey.

Page 25: Students will need to access holiday brochures to complete this activity.

Build your learning

It may be possible to arrange for students to visit a holiday centre, such as Butlin's or Center Parcs. Because this topic is split over two sessions, it may also be useful to summarise the key factors that have led to the development of the travel and tourism industry at the end of this session. Following this session students could also be given the end of section activity, as this forms part of the portfolio assessment.

Session 4

Textbook pages 29 to 33

Resources required

- OHT 2
- Financial pages of any national broadsheet newspaper
- Examples of objectives of public and private sector travel and tourism organisations

Objectives of session

- To identify and discuss the key features of the travel and tourism industry, covering:
  (a) private sector
  (b) public sector
  (c) voluntary sector
  (d) use of new technology.

Development of textbook

- A useful starting point could be to use OHT 2 to provide an overview of the key features of the travel and tourism industry.
- Cover each of the three sectors by providing definitions and examples of organisations within each sector. This could be further developed by holding a group discussion about the contrasting objectives of selected organisations from each sector. You could use the case study about the BTA on page 59 as a public sector example.
- You may also find it useful to use information from Unit 4 (pages 229 to 231) about marketing objectives of travel and tourism organisations. Alternatively you might be able to access this information via the internet (look, for example, at www.tourismconcern.org.uk, www.british-airways.com, www.englishtourism.org.uk) or from annual company reports.
- Use of technology should also have been covered in session 2. Remind students about the influence of developing transport and communications technologies on the travel and tourism industry. You could use the case study on page 33 to provide an example of a global distribution system.

Key words to define

Commercial and non-commercial, private sector, public limited companies, shareholders, public sector, voluntary sector, global distribution systems.

Answers to textbook activities

Page 29: This information could be obtained from the internet or from publicity materials, holiday brochures and company reports for each of the listed organisations.

Build your learning

Guest speakers representing organisations from each sector could provide information about their objectives and business activities. It may also be possible to arrange a group visit to one of the major travel fairs.

Session 5

Textbook pages 33 to 38

Resources required

- OHT 2
- North Yorks Moors National Park case study (pages 134 to 135)

Objectives of session

- To recap on previous session.
- To identify and discuss the key features of the travel and tourism industry, covering:
  (e) external pressures
  (f) impact on host communities.

Development of textbook

- Use OHT 2 to recap on the features covered in the previous session and highlight the two key features that are the focus of this session: external pressures and the impact of tourism on host communities.
- Page 33 of the textbook gives six examples of external pressures that could cause problems for the travel and tourism industry. You can draw from the examples shown on pages 33 to 35 of the textbook to illustrate the vulnerability of the industry to these external pressures.
- You could develop this further by adding more recent examples, such as the poor weather for most of summer 2000 in Britain, or the threat of war in the Middle East.
- The positive and negative impacts of tourism on host communities is also covered in Unit 2, pages 130 to 142. In this session, the emphasis should be on providing an overview of the main types of impact – economic, social and cultural – rather than detailed analysis. You might find it useful to use some of the examples and case study material from Unit 2. The North York Moors case study and activity on pages 134 to 135 could be used to generate group discussion.

Key words to define

Host community, multiplier effect, economic impact, social impact, environmental impact, sustainable tourism, ecotourism.

Build your learning

Because this topic is split over two sessions, it may be useful to summarise the key features of the travel and tourism industry at the end of this session. Following this session students could also be given the end of section activity on page 38 of the textbook, as this forms part of the portfolio assessment.

Session 6

Textbook pages 39 to 44

Resources required

- OHT 3 and 4
- Information about a selection of travel agencies such as company annual reports and publicity materials
- Handout of Figure 1.14, page 41, and case study, page 43.

There is also a large amount of information about the major travel agency chains available on the internet. The Yellow Pages could also be used to find a list of travel agencies in a particular area.

Objectives of session

- To investigate the structure of the UK travel and tourism industry.
- To provide an overview of the six key industry components.
- To review the supply structure and chain of distribution.
- To investigate:
  (a) travel agencies.

Development of textbook

- Introduce the session by using OHT 3 and 4 to show the six key industry components and the chain of distribution in the travel and tourism industry. It may also be useful to provide students with definitions of the components and other key terms such as principals and vertical integration.
- Examples of organisations within each component of the industry and at each stage of the chain of distribution should be provided. It is important that students understand that these components are often interrelated. There are also obvious links with the leisure and recreation industry.
- You might find it useful to introduce the travel agency industry component by explaining the difference between retail and business agencies. Use Figure 1.14 to provide students with a list of the top twenty ABTA retail travel agencies.
- Students need to be aware that retail travel agencies may operate as independent outlets or form part of a multiple or miniple chain. You can use the case study on page 43 to show how the process of integration has affected this industry component.
- Provide students with examples of business travel agencies and explain what services they offer to their clients. You can use the press article on page 45 to illustrate the benefits of using specialist business travel consultants.

Key words to define

Supply structure, chain of distribution, principals, vertical integration, producers, wholesalers, retailers, retail travel agencies, independent outlets, multiples, miniples, business travel agencies.

Answers to textbook activities

Page 44 'The supply structure in retail travel': The benefits are that tour operators can sell their products directly to customers through their high street agencies. They can also ensure that their products are given prominent display within the shops, and priority from the sales consultants. They can also undercut competitors by offering greater discounts on their own products. In some cases, the independents have had to concentrate on selling holiday products offered by the smaller tour operators. They have found it difficult to compete with the integrated companies on price, so they tend to offer more specialist travel services, such as bespoke packages or niche market holidays.

Information for task 3 can be obtained from a Yellow Pages directory. For task 4, students should note that if more and more people use the internet to book holidays direct from tour operators, it is likely that the number of high street travel agencies will reduce significantly. This has already happened in other industries, such as banking, where automation and 'plastic' payment has eliminated the need for extensive branch networks.

Page 44 'Business travel agencies': The main advantages are that specialist business travel agencies can be more cost effective, more efficient, have larger buying power, use CRS to find best deals, provide specialist travel advice, and offer specialist travel management services for large companies.

Build your learning

It may be possible to invite a guest speaker from a retail or business travel agency.

Session 7

Textbook pages 44 to 53

Resources required

- OHT 3 and 4
- Information about a selection of travel agencies such as company annual reports and publicity materials
- Handout of Figure 1.15, page 47, and the case studies on pages 46, 49 and 52
- Selection of brochures covering the holiday types listed in the activity on page 48

There is also a large amount of information about the major tour operators available on the internet. The Yellow Pages could also be used to find a list of tour operators in a particular area.

Objectives of session

- To investigate:
  (b) tour operations.

Development of textbook

- OHT 3 provides an overview of the six key components that make up the UK travel and tourism industry. It is important that students understand that the travel agency and tour operation components are closely related.
- You could use OHT 4 to remind students of the supply chain. There are also obvious links between tour operations and all the other components.
- You might find it useful to introduce the tour operations industry component by explaining the difference between outbound, inbound and domestic tour operators.
- You can use Figure 1.15 to provide students with a list of the top twenty UK tour operators in terms of passengers carried in 1999.
- The activity on page 48 can be used to help students identify well-known tour operator brands.
- You can use the Airtours case study on page 49 to show an example of a major tour operator that has achieved both vertical and horizontal integration.
- You might want to provide students with examples of inbound and domestic tour operators. The case study on page 52 provides some examples of domestic tour operators. This could be supported by showing students examples of holiday brochures provided by these operators.

Key words to define

Tour operators, outbound tour operators, horizontal integration, inbound tour operators, domestic tour operators.

Answers to textbook activities

To compete the activities in this session, students will need an appropriate range of holiday brochures. Students should be able to complete all of the tasks using brochures or by accessing tour operator websites on the internet.

Build your learning

It may be possible to invite a guest speaker from a tour operator. If you have access to the internet, it may be possible for students to gather information about the major tour operators through their websites. Some website addresses are provided on page 464 of the textbook.

Session 8

Textbook pages 53 to 58

Resources required

- OHT 3

- Handouts for Figure 1.17, page 53, for Figure 1.19, page 56, and for the map on page 54
- To complete the activity on page 54, students will need travel atlases or ferry brochures, Yellow Pages, and local 'where to eat' and accommodation guides

Objectives of session

- To investigate:
  (c) transport
  (d) accommodation and catering.

Development of textbook

- Recap previous session by using OHT 3. Give examples of links between transport, accommodation and catering and the other components.
- As an introduction to the transport component, it could be useful to outline the various transport categories. Use Figure 1.17, page 53, to provide an example of the volume of traffic at the UK's main airports. The activity on page 54 can be used to locate the main UK airports and seaports. Students will need travel atlases or ferry brochures to identify the main ferry routes.
- Introduce the accommodation and catering component by defining the different types of accommodation. You can use Figure 1.20 to show students the largest UK hotel groups in 1998. You might be able to provide examples of different types of accommodation provider and catering establishment from your own locality.
- Identify the many links between catering and the other components. Provide students with examples of the wide range of catering operations and establishments. You can use the press article on page 58 to provide students with information about the size of the restaurant market.

Key words to define

Transport carrier, terminal, accommodation provider, catering establishment.

Answers to textbook activities

Page 54: The answers to this activity can be obtained from a travel atlas or from ferry brochures.

Page 57: The range of products and services offered by an accommodation provider can often be obtained from its publicity materials or brochures. Alternatively, it may be provided by a local TIC in its accommodation guide.

Page 58: A list of catering establishments for a particular locality can usually be obtained from the Yellow Pages. Many TICs, and some hotels, also produce 'where to eat' guides for their localities.

Build your learning

You could arrange a group visit to a transport, accommodation or catering facility, such as an airport, ferry port or hotel.

Session 9

Textbook pages 58 to 66

Resources required

- OHT 3
- Handouts for BTA case study, page 59, and for Figures 1.21, 1.22, 1.23, 1.24, 1.25 and 1.26
- Leaflets or posters about tourist attractions and road touring maps are required for the activity on page 62

Internet access is required for the activities on pages 64 and 65. See the textbook's internet directory for national park websites. For further details of visitor numbers to tourist attractions visit www.staruk.org.uk.

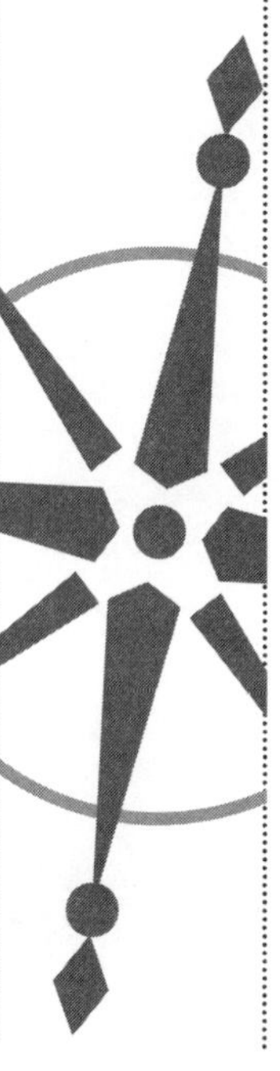

Objectives of session

- To investigate:
  (e) tourism development
  (f) tourist attractions.
- To recap on previous sessions about the six components.

Development of textbook

- Recap previous session by using OHT 3. In this session, students will learn about the final two components of the industry: tourism development and tourist attractions.
- Introduce tourism development by explaining what it involves and giving examples of the agents involved in tourism development. You can use the case study about the role of the BTA to provide one example (page 59).
- Use the ETC definition of tourist attraction to introduce this component. You can use Figures 1.21, 1.22, 1.23, 1.24. 1.25 and 1.26 from pages 60 to 64 to show the most popular facilities within the main categories of tourist attraction.
- Further information is available via the staruk website. You may find it useful to provide publicity materials, posters, leaflets, etc. for some of the attractions identified.
- You will need to provide students with road and tourist maps to complete the activity on page 62 of the textbook. Students will ideally have internet access to complete the activities on pages 64 and 65. These activities could also involve visits to the attraction.
- As this session is the last of the four sessions devoted to explaining the structure of the industry, it may be useful to allow some additional time for a recap.

Key words to define

Guiding services, visitor/tourist attraction, theme park, museum.

Build your learning

After this session students could be given the end of section activity on page 66. This could form part of their portfolio of evidence. This session could be supported by visits to tourist attractions such as theme parks, museums, national parks, stately homes, etc.

Session 10

Textbook pages 67 to 71

Resources required

- Handouts of Figures 1.27 to 1.35
- *ETC Sightseeing in the UK 1999*
- *Social Trends*
- *Annual Abstract of Statistics*
- *Employment Gazette*

Information can also be obtained from the internet. For economic data and employment statistics, for example, visit www.ons.gov.uk, www.statistics.gov.uk and www.keynote.co.uk.

Objectives of session

- To identify and discuss the scale and significance of the UK travel and tourism industry in terms of:
  (a) consumer spending and contribution to the balance of payments
  (b) numbers employed nationally
  (c) number of tourists coming into the UK
  (d) number of domestic and outgoing tourists.

Development of textbook

- Use Figures 1.27, 1.28, 1.29, 1.30 and 1.31 on pages 67 and 68 of the textbook to show the economic value of tourism in the UK economy, as measured by the BTA/ETC.
- You may also find it useful to provide statistics from other market research organisations such as Mintel, LIRC and Keynote. It is important that students understand the term balance of payments, and how the tourism industry contributes to the UK's balance of payments.
- Figure 1.32 provides data on the number of people employed in tourism. You could develop this by investigating employment trends in your own locality to illustrate the importance of the industry to the local economy.
- Figures 1.33, 1.34 and 1.35 can be used to provide students with statistics about the numbers and distribution of tourists.

Key words to define

Direct and indirect income, multiplier effect, balance of payments, employment statistics, participation trends, and cultural and social significance.

Answers to textbook activities

Page 69 'Tourism's balance of payments': Suggested answers to each task are:

- outbound tourism increases, inbound decreases – there is a negative impact on balance of payments
- outbound tourism decreases, inbound increases – there is a positive impact on balance of payments
- increase in domestic tourism, particularly short breaks – positive impact on balance of payments
- fewer visitors from USA to the UK and vice-versa – probable negative impact on balance of payments
- increase in domestic and outbound tourism – likely minimal change to balance of payments.

Build your learning

Students could be given the end of section activity on page 71 of the textbook. This forms part of the portfolio evidence for this unit.

Session 11

Textbook pages 72 to 79

Resources required

- OHT 5
- Situations vacant sections of local newspapers
- Examples of job descriptions and person specifications
- Internet sites such as www.careercompass.co.uk, www.ilam.co.uk and www.sprito.org.uk

Objectives of session

- To identify and discuss the range of employment opportunities in travel and tourism.
- To identify the type of personal and technical skills required by employers.

Development of textbook

- Use OHT 5 to provide examples of the wide range of employment opportunities available in the industry. Figure 1.37 (on page 76) can be used to illustrate the progression opportunities from operative to management positions.
- It may be possible to draw upon the work experiences of students within the group to discuss the nature of employment in the industry, such as unsocial hours, shift work, etc. If not, you could use case studies or invite visiting speakers (perhaps ex-students) to tell students about their work.
- Information provided by employers, or examples of job descriptions and person specifications can be used to illustrate the range of personal qualities and skills needed by those wishing to work in the industry.

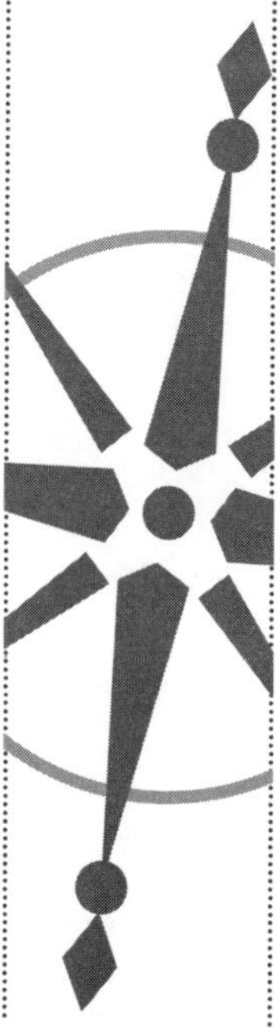

Key words to define

Job description, person specification, personal attributes, personal qualities, personal achievements, vocational qualifications and competence.

Answers to textbook activities

Page 75: You may need to provide students with job descriptions and person specifications for task 3.

Page 76: For task 2, you may be able to obtain examples to show how employers compensate employees for working unsocial hours. Examples include enhanced pay, overtime, shift bonuses, provision of meals, transport home after shift, living-in facility, employee share schemes and staff discounts.

Page 77: The hotel manager provided comment 3, holiday resort rep is comment 6, travel sales consultant is comment 4, a tour guide is comment 2, skiing instructor is comment 1, and the air cabin crew is comment 5.

Build your learning

Your school/college may have careers advice and publications that could be useful when delivering this session. Check out if there are any relevant careers or jobs fairs in your locality. Some of the major employers also produce student information packs about applying for jobs.

Session 12

Textbook pages 79 to 85

Resources required

- Handouts of case study on page 81
- Situations vacant sections of local newspapers
- Examples of job descriptions and person specifications
- Internet sites www.careercompass.co.uk and www.ilam.co.uk

Objectives of session

- To investigate sources of information about jobs in travel and tourism.
- To identify jobs that match students' interests, skills, qualifications and aspirations.

Development of textbook

- Introduce the session by highlighting the main sources of information about jobs in travel and tourism. This could be delivered by a member of the careers team at your school/college. You could obtain examples of key industry publications such as *Travel Weekly*, *Travel Trade Gazette*, ILAM and newspapers to show where and how jobs are advertised.
- You could use the case study on page 81, or invite visiting speakers, to provide some illustrative job profiles. Alternatively, students could interview people currently working in the industry about their jobs.
- Students need to be made aware about the vast range of job information that is available on the internet on employer websites and specialist job recruitment sites.
- In the final part of the session, students should be encouraged to identify suitable jobs based on their own aspirations and circumstances. Once this has been done, each student should be given advice about the training, qualifications, skills and experience that will be required for the jobs that they have identified.

Answers to textbook activities

Page 82: This may be possible to undertake as part of a work placement programme.

Build your learning

Following this session students should be able to complete the end of section activity on page 85 of the textbook. This may provide evidence for the portfolio assessment.

Session 13

Textbook pages 86 to 93

Resources required

- Sample application forms
- Access to IT facilities and word processing packages

Objectives of session

- To provide practical tips and advice on how to apply for jobs; covering letters of application, application forms and interview skills.

Development of textbook

- Provide students with examples of letters of application. It might be useful to provide some examples that contain mistakes and then ask students to identify and correct them.
- Students could be provided with actual job adverts that they could apply for in writing. They could be asked to produce their letters of application by word processor.
- Provide students with copies of sample job application forms to complete. This could be made more realistic by liaising with a local employer to use real life examples.
- This session could be developed by holding mock interviews for the jobs that students have applied for in the writing exercises.

Key words to define

Letters of application, application form, interview.

Build your learning

It may be possible to involve local employers in mock interviews. This would help prepare students for the real thing.

Session 14

Textbook pages 90 to 93

Resources required

- OHT 6
- Sample CV layouts
- Access to IT facilities and word processing packages

Objectives of session

- To provide guidance on what to include in, and how to present, a CV.

Development of textbook

- Introduce session by explaining the term CV. Outline how CVs can be used. OHT 6 can be used to show students what should be included in a CV.
- Provide students with examples of CVs. It might be useful to provide some examples that contain mistakes and then ask students to identify and correct them.
- It may be possible to provide students with a template on a computer disk so that they can put together their own CVs.
- Suggest possible layout and content for a covering letter to accompany students' CVs.

Key words to define

Curriculum vitae.

Build your learning

Following this session students should be able to complete the end of section activity on page 93 of the textbook. This may provide evidence for their portfolio assessment.

Session 15

Textbook pages 452 to 453

Resources required

- Handout of portfolio assessment for the unit

Objectives of session

- To consolidate the learning from the previous 14 sessions.
- To discuss and coordinate the assessment evidence for the unit.

Development of textbook

- This session might be introduced by recapping the key areas and words that have been defined and used throughout this unit. The unit content page on page 3 of the textbook can be used to provide a summary of the content of the 14 sessions. Tutors might like to create a short quiz and ask student teams to define a selection of the key words given in each session.
- Tutors will need to spend some time explaining the unit assessment evidence requirements and how grades are decided.
- For part one of the assessment, students need to undertake a group or individual investigation into the UK travel and tourism industry covering the areas shown on page 452 (tasks 1 to 4). End of section activities on textbook pages 28, 38, 66 and 71 could be used to generate portfolio evidence for these tasks.
- Part two of the assessment must be completed by students on an individual basis as it involves identifying a suitable job based on their own circumstances and producing a CV. Part 2 is shown on page 453, tasks 5 to 7. End of section activities on pages 85 and 93 could be used to generate portfolio evidence for these tasks.

Development of the UK travel and tourism industry

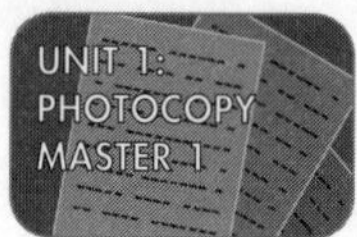

Key factors that have led to the postwar growth of the travel and tourism industry

Changing socioeconomic circumstances

Increases in leisure time, disposable income and car ownership

Technological developments

Jet aircraft, use of computers, the internet

Product development and innovation

Package holidays, long haul, all-inclusives, Christmas, short breaks

Changing consumer needs, expectations and fashions

Short-break holidays, independent travel, long-haul exotic destinations

UNIT 1: PHOTOCOPY MASTER 2

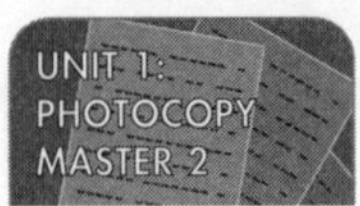

Key features of the travel and tourism industry

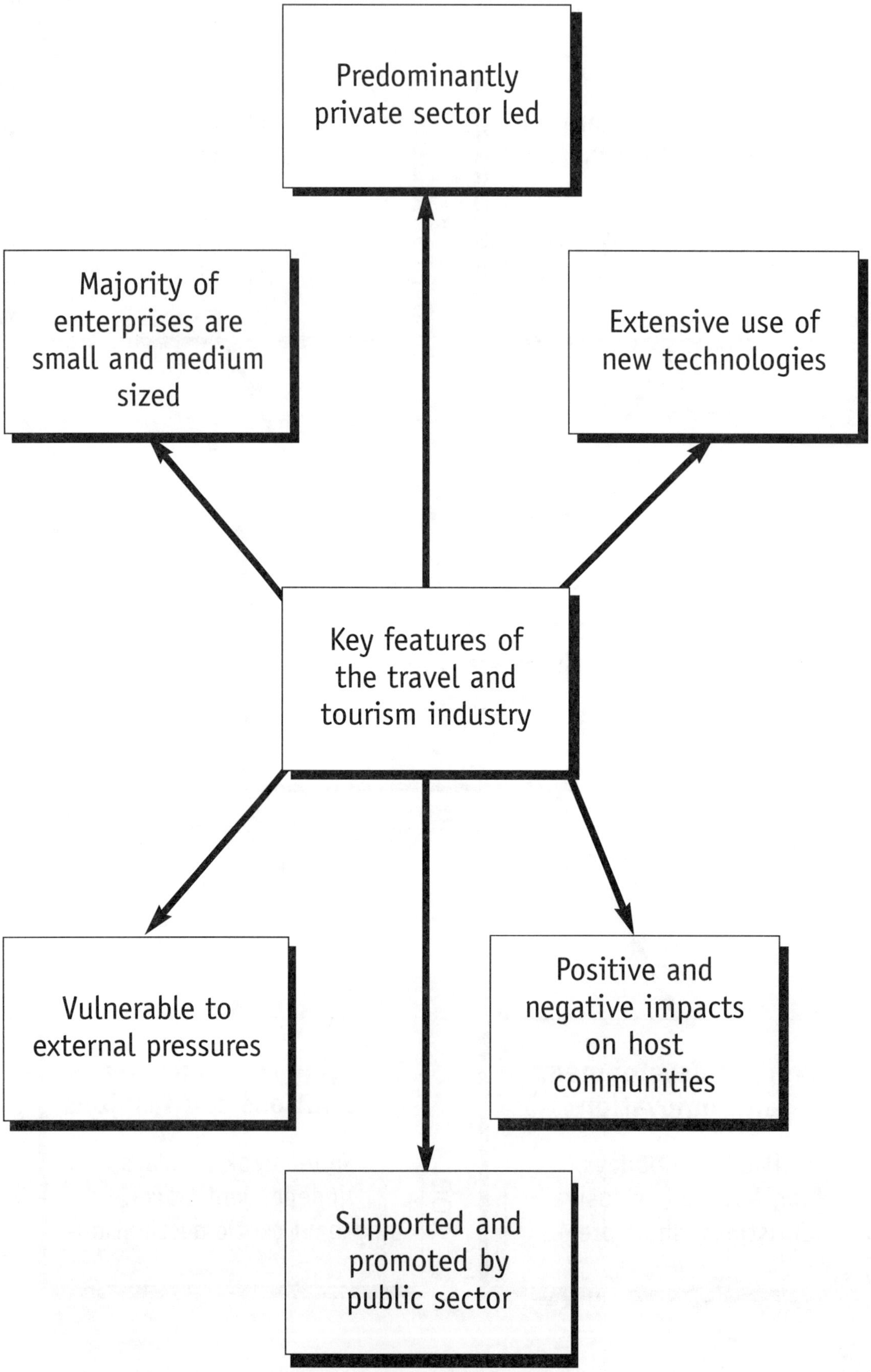

Predominantly private sector led
Majority of enterprises are small and medium sized
Extensive use of new technologies
Key features of the travel and tourism industry
Vulnerable to external pressures
Positive and negative impacts on host communities
Supported and promoted by public sector

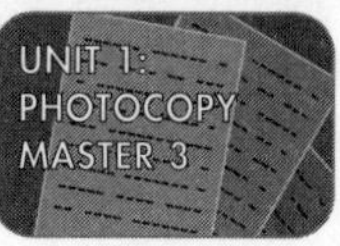

Key components of the travel and tourism industry

UNIT 1:
PHOTOCOPY
MASTER 3

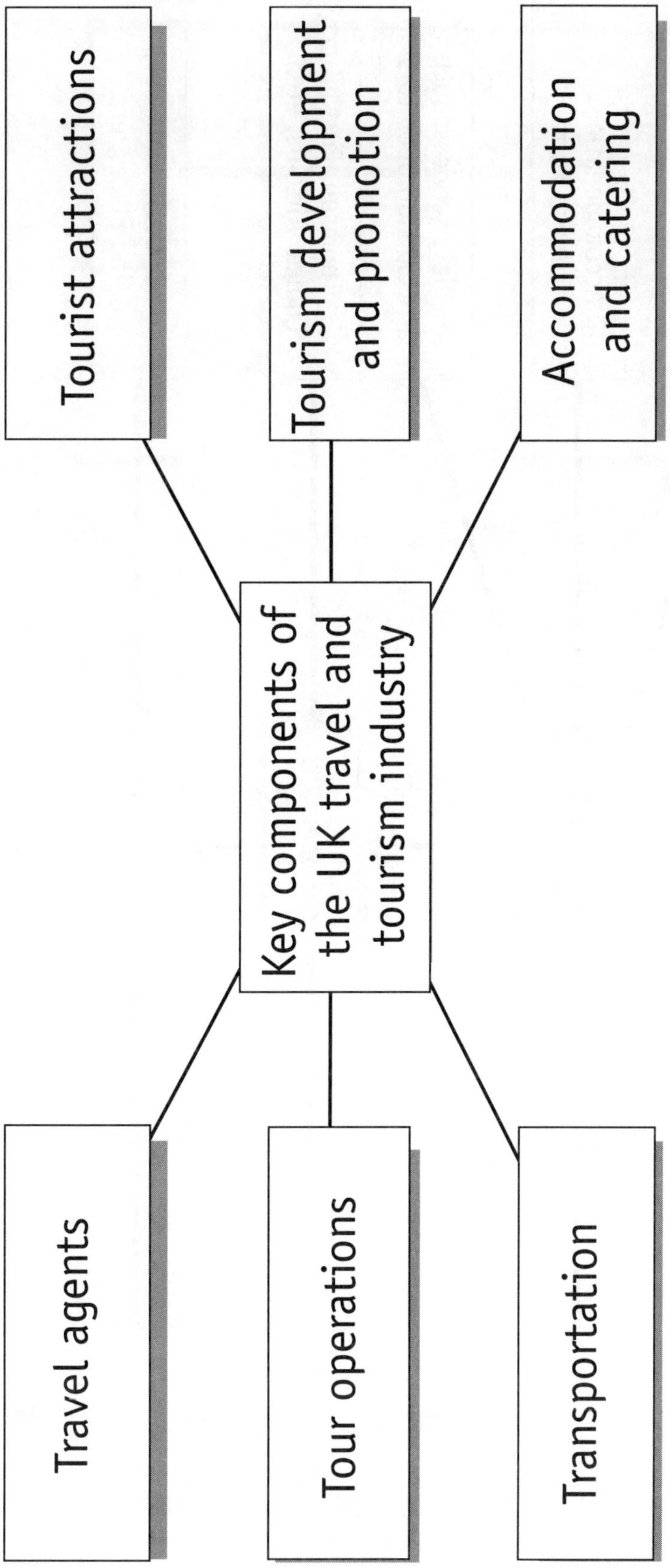

Tourist attractions
Tourism development and promotion
Accommodation and catering
Key components of the UK travel and tourism industry
Travel agents
Tour operations
Transportation

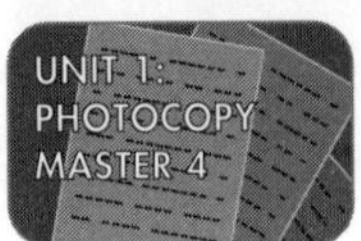

Chain of distribution in the travel and tourism industry

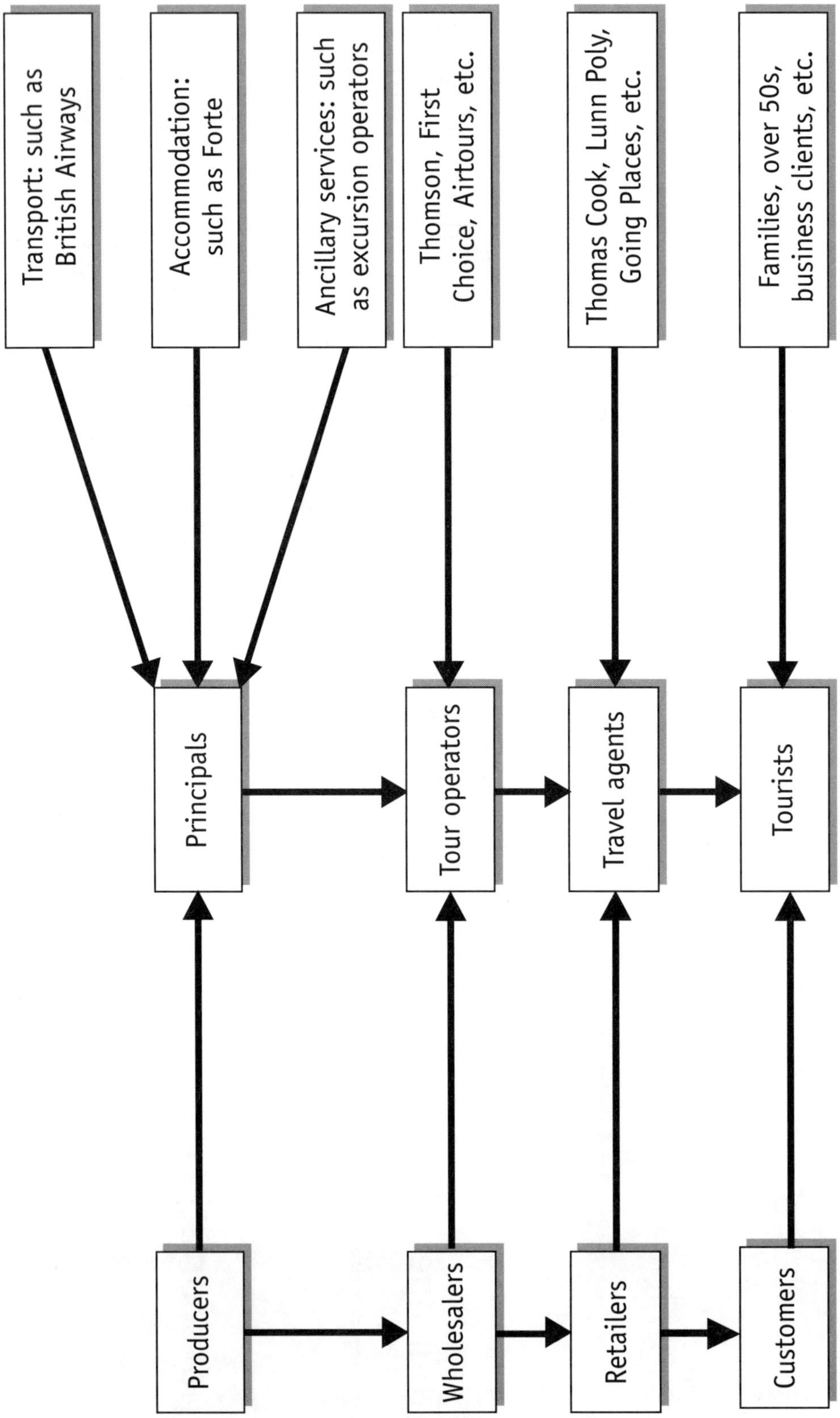

Producers → Principals ← Transport: such as British Airways; Accommodation: such as Forte; Ancillary services: such as excursion operators

Wholesalers → Tour operators ← Thomson, First Choice, Airtours, etc.

Retailers → Travel agents ← Thomas Cook, Lunn Poly, Going Places, etc.

Customers → Tourists ← Families, over 50s, business clients, etc.

Producers → Wholesalers → Retailers → Customers

Principals → Tour operators → Travel agents → Tourists

Examples of jobs in the travel and tourism industry

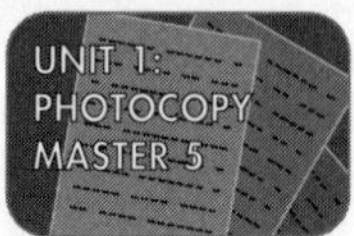

Travel agents

- Sales consultant
- Assistant shop manager
- Shop manager
- Business travel consultant
- Currency exchange cashier

Tour operators

- Resort representative
- Travel courier
- Administrator
- Bookings/sales consultant
- Marketing officer

Transportation

- Air cabin crew
- Customer service advisor
- Retail sales consultant
- Technical maintenance jobs
- Security
- Baggage handler

Tourist attractions

- Front-of-house manager
- Receptionist
- Retail sales
- Tour guide
- Entertainer
- Education officer

Tourism development and promotion

- Tourist information centre advisor
- Marketing officer
- Education officer
- Tourist board marketing and promotions staff
- Event organiser

Accommodation and catering

- Waiter/waitress
- Barperson
- Front of house manager/ receptionist
- Chef
- Housekeeper
- Administrator
- Booking/sales consultant

What to include in a CV

Personal details	Age, marital status , address and telephone number.
Academic and vocational qualifications	Details of school and colleges attended, dates subjects studied and grades obtained plus details of qualifications you are currently pursuing.
Employment/work experience	Details of previous employment, including part-time, full-time and voluntary work. Give brief details of your duties and responsibilities and any specialist skills used.
Achievements and other qualifications	For example, driving license, first aid certificate, lifesaving awards.
Personal interests	Leisure activities, pastimes, memberships of clubs or societies. Highlight activities that show initiative and responsibility.
References	The names of two referees, with addresses, identifying in what capacity they know you, for example 'youth leader' manager of office during my work experience placement.

Unit 2:
Tourism development

Introduction

This unit examines and evaluates the agents involved in tourism development and describes the various strategies that are employed to ensure that the positive impacts of development are maximised while negative impacts are minimised. Students should develop a sound understanding and appreciation of both short-term and long-term development issues and the considerable responsibilities that tourism development encompasses.

Delivery suggestions

Due to its global context, this unit involves a large amount of detailed taught content. Tutors should avoid focusing too frequently on domestic issues. Although these are clearly relevant, students also need to appreciate and understand international tourism development issues. This is particularly important in terms of preparing students for the external unit assessment.

Case studies are often the best way of allowing students to consider and evaluate the different issues involved and the text contains a wide range of examples. Further examples are readily available on the internet and in travel and tourism journals. Students should also be encouraged to report back to the group on any tourism development issues that they have identified in newspaper articles and television reports and documentaries. Organised visits and guest speakers will enhance students' understanding of tourism development.

Links to other units

Unit 1

Tourism development has strong links to investigating travel and tourism in terms of exploring the ways in which the various sectors of the industry have been developed and reviewing the agents responsible for the development.

Unit 3

Students' knowledge and understanding of worldwide travel destinations will provide a firm foundation when evaluating and comparing the development issues in different countries. For example, the travel file on Benidorm on page 203 of the textbook can be used to supplement the tourism development case study on page 149 of the textbook.

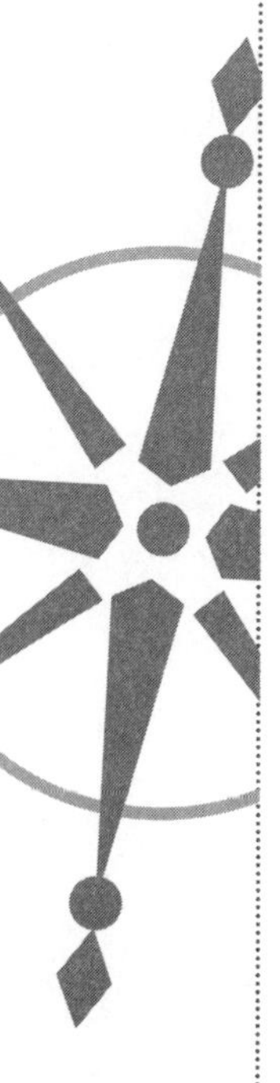

Unit 4

Students should consider the importance of marketing in tourism development. Issues such as product development, attracting new customers, targeting, position in the product life cycle, market research and marketing communications might be explored.

Unit planner

Session	Session objectives	Text pages
1	To introduce the unit To identify and discuss the various agents of tourism development within private sector enterprises	96 to 98
2	To identify and discuss the various agents of tourism development within the public sector	98 to 103
3	To identify and discuss the various agents of tourism development within the voluntary sector	104 to 106
4	To identify and discuss the economic objectives of tourism development	107 to 111
5	To identify and discuss the environmental objectives of tourism development	112 to 117
6	To identify and discuss the sociocultural objectives of tourism development	118 to 123
7	To identify and discuss the political objectives of tourism development	124 to 129
8	To identify and discuss the economic impacts of tourism development	130 to 133
9	To identify and discuss the environmental impacts of tourism development	133 to 135
10	To identify and discuss the sociocultural impacts of tourism development	136 to 142
11	To identify and discuss how the positive impacts of tourism development can be maximised	143 to 146
12	To identify and discuss how the negative impacts of tourism development can be minimised through planning control and the principles of sustainable tourism	147 to 150
13	To identify and discuss how the negative impacts of tourism development can be minimised through visitor and traffic management	150 to 151
14	To identify and discuss how the negative impacts of tourism development can be minimised through environmental impact assessments and environmental audits	151 to 155
15	To prepare for the external unit assessment	

Session 1

Textbook pages 96 to 98

Resources required

- OHT 1

Objectives of session

- To introduce the unit.
- To identify and discuss the various agents of tourism development within private sector enterprises.

Development of textbook

- This session might be introduced by giving students a brief summary of topics covered by the unit.
- You might ask students to brainstorm to produce a list of agents that are involved in the development of tourism. Ideas can be listed on the whiteboard in three columns. Column headings of 'private', 'public' and 'voluntary' can be added at the end of the exercise. The range of tourism development agents can be summarised using OHT 1.
- When discussing private sector enterprises, students might be asked to identify the specific sectors of the industry that are predominantly developed by the private sector. Answers might include the hospitality industry, travel agencies and tour operations.
- The topic of development agencies is best explained by giving students real examples, such as USM which is described in the case study on page 97 of the textbook. Students might consider which other agents a development agency is likely to be involved with in its day-to-day work.
- When discussing landowners, students might consider the rapid growth of rural and farm tourism products and be asked to identify specific products within this sector such as camping and caravan sites, craft outlets, etc.
- Students should be able to name a range of private sector organisations in each of the six leisure and entertainment categories listed on page 98 of the textbook. This might be extended into a research activity with students finding out the top three providers in each category.

Key words to define

Tourism development, agents, private sector enterprises, development agencies, landowners, leisure and entertainment organisations.

Answers to textbook activities

Page 98: As an alternative to this activity, students might be asked to suggest a tourism development project that could be initiated locally and to discuss which private sector enterprises would need to be involved. They should also consider where the project would be sited and which landowners might be involved in the development.

Build your learning

The National Centre for Popular Music in Sheffield (see page 96) and the Earth Centre in Doncaster (pages 114 to 116) both represent large-scale tourism development projects. However, in the summer of 2000 both attractions announced that they were closing. Students might investigate the reasons why these attractions were forced to close.

Session 2

Textbook pages 98 to 103

Resources required

- OHT 1
- Access to the internet

Objectives of session

- To identify and discuss the various agents of tourism development within the public sector.

Development of textbook

- This session can be introduced by reminding students of the agents involved in tourism development using OHT 1.
- It is important that students are provided with a range of examples of both domestic and overseas government agencies. They need to understand that government agencies in different countries can have different objectives when deciding on tourism development policies.
- When discussing the role of local authorities it is useful for students to acquire a detailed knowledge of how tourism development is supported and initiated locally. Figures on the allocation of budgets for tourism development are available from local authorities. Students might discuss the extent to which they agree with this allocation.
- Detailed information on the regional development agencies is available on the Department of the Environment, Transport and the Regions' (DETR) website (www.detr.gov.uk). Students can investigate the ways in which the regional development agency for their area contributes to tourism development.
- Students examined the role of the national and regional tourist boards in Unit 1. Within this unit, it is important that they can distinguish between the various roles that the boards have in tourism development. Figure 2.2 on page 103 of the textbook can help them to understand the relationship between the various public sector bodies in the UK.

Key words to define

Public sector organisations, central government, overseas governments, Department for Culture, Media and Sport (DCMS), local authorities, regional development agencies, English Tourism Council, national tourist boards, regional tourist boards.

Answers to textbook activities

Page 99: Tutors might allocate one organisation to individual students or small groups and ask each to report back their findings.

Page 100 'The DCMS': This is usually a contentious issue and students may be surprised to discover how much money is allocated to minority interests such as opera.

Page 100 'Industrial cities': Where access permits, it will be valuable for students to visit and evaluate an industrial city or town that has been developed as a tourist destination.

Build your learning

Using the case study on page 102 as a starting point, students might investigate in more depth the agents involved in the development of farm tourism in the UK. For example, they might identify the sources of funding and grants available to farmers wishing to develop a tourism product.

Session 3

Textbook pages 104 to 106

Resources required

- OHT 1
- Access to the internet

Objectives of session

- To identify and discuss the various agents of tourism development within the voluntary sector.

Development of textbook

- This session can be introduced by recapping on the agents involved in tourism development using OHT 1. Build on the list of voluntary sector bodies that students brainstormed during session 1.
- It is useful for students to discover the vast amount of information available about voluntary sector tourism development agents on the internet. Two particularly useful sites are Tourism Concern (www. tourismconcern.org.uk) and VSO (www. vso.org.uk). The information on these sites provides a relevant and current insight into many tourism development issues and is particularly important in developing students' awareness of tourism development in different countries. You might like to allow students some time to access these two websites and collect some information on international tourism agents. In preparation for sessions 8 to 10, students can be asked to identify some of the key impacts of tourism development in different countries.
- As a conclusion to the session, emphasise that the three sectors of tourism development agents – private, public and voluntary – are interdependent and closely linked. Students should be asked to give examples of this interdependency.

Key words to define

Voluntary sector bodies, community groups, pressure groups.

Answers to textbook activities

Page 104: This activity requires adequate preparation time if it is to be useful. Students should be given sufficient time to research further information and prepare their arguments. Using 'Zenith project, Scarborough' as a search phrase on the internet will provide students with a number of websites that contain a range of opinions and up-to-date information on the project.

You might also like to use the activity to provide an opportunity for students to familiarise themselves with – and use – the basic procedures that are customary in a formal meeting, such as addressing all comments through the chair. There are numerous opportunities for collecting evidence for key skills in communication. This can be enhanced if students also write up the minutes of the meeting using an appropriate format and style.

Page 106: For the end of section activity, tutors might arrange for a guest speaker from the local authority to talk to the students about tourism development within the area.

Build your learning

In preparation for the next session students can be asked to think about the key objectives of the tourism development agents involved in the Zenith project.

Session 4

Textbook pages 107 to 111

Resources required

- OHT 2
- Access to the internet

Objectives of session

- To identify and discuss the economic objectives of tourism development.

Development of textbook

- If students have undertaken the build your learning activity suggested for the last session, you might ask them to discuss the objectives that they have identified. Prompt students to ensure that they provide examples from the four categories – economic, environmental, sociocultural and political – of objectives. For example, if students have not provided any environmental examples, ask them to consider Richard Smith's comment that the site is 'desperately in need of up-grade and improvement'.

- The range of tourism development objectives can be summarised using OHT 2. Students should be asked to consider and suggest the ways in which tourism development can result in economic gain. Suggestions may be summarised using the four bullet points on page 107 of the textbook.
- Students might suggest which of the four economic gains derived from tourism development are likely to be main objectives of particular tourism development agents. For example, central government and local authorities might be concerned about job creation; private sector enterprises would usually put increased income as a primary objective. However, students should be aware that an organisation might well have all of these objectives in undertaking tourism development. For example, a private sector enterprise often cites job creation as one of its objectives because this can result in increased support from public and voluntary sector agents.

Key words to define

Economic objectives, economic gain, job creation, foreign currency earnings, leakage, domestic spending, increasing income and profitability, economic development and regeneration.

Answers to textbook activities

Page 109: It is crucial that students understand the concept of tourism leakage; they should not view all tourism development as positive simply because it generates a large amount of revenue. The concept also impacts on sociocultural issues and can be revisited in later sessions. Relevant responses to the case study will include that tourism leakage occurs because:

- the higher paid staff in all-inclusive hotels may be expatriates – for example, international hotel companies and tour operators may employ foreign nationals
- guests spend little on local products and services because everything is included in the price and many do not venture out of the hotel complexes
- the basic commodities used may be imported rather than local – for example, the bars and restaurants of all-inclusive resorts stock many branded spirits and soft drinks imported from the USA and Europe.

Page 110: Students can gain a greater understanding of the Portsmouth Harbour Renaissance project by visiting the website at www.gosport.gov.uk/development/millennium/elements

Build your learning

In preparation for session 6 students might consider the impact that all-inclusive holidays, and the subsequent tourism leakage, might have on the host community.

Session 5

Textbook pages 112 to 117

Resources required

- OHT 2

Objectives of session

- To identify and discuss the environmental objectives of tourism development.

Development of textbook

- This session should be introduced by reminding students of the objectives of tourism development using OHT 2. Students might then be asked to consider the ways in which tourism development can effect the environment and, therefore, what general environmental objectives tourism development agents might set. Ideas can be summarised under the three bullet points on page 113 of the textbook.
- Tutors might invite a guest speaker from a local organisation or pressure group to talk to students about the effect that tourism development can have on wildlife. Students need to be aware that established habitats and breeding grounds (of any form of wildlife) can often prohibit development

- When discussing environmental improvements students need to appreciate the full range of definitions that the term encompasses. For example, it does not necessarily mean restoring the environment to its state before decline. Many factors, such as costs and society's needs, have to be considered when identifying what constitutes environmental improvement. For example, the Zenith project featured on page 105 of the textbook would result in considerable changes to the existing physical environment yet, arguably, delivers environmental improvement.

Key words to define

Environmental objectives, preservation of wildlife, environmental education, environmental improvements.

Answers to textbook activities

Page 114 'Zakinthos': Students might suggest a visitor attraction that encompasses a turtle sanctuary similar to the seal and otter sanctuaries operated by Vardon Attractions' Sealife Centres. Such an attraction might include video footage of the turtles in their natural habitat as well as educational materials and displays.

Page 114 'The Earth Centre, Doncaster': The topic of sustainability is studied in depth in session 12. However, it is useful for students to familiarise themselves with the term at this stage and attempt to identify and collect examples of sustainable tourism initiatives. You should inform students that the Earth Centre in Doncaster has now closed.

Page 116 'Tourism and environmental damage': Students might consider the unfortunate fact that many tourists' perception of the lack of damage is based on their own needs rather than an overall appreciation of the existing environment. For example, holidaymakers going to the Greek islands may welcome a proliferation of amusements arcades, English pubs, fast-food restaurants and high-rise hotels. They may not consider that these developments damage the natural environment simply because they like the facilities.

Page 116 'Environmental improvements': Students might identify some of the following methods:

- setting out to attract people who are environmentally aware and therefore want to preserve the existing environment
- using natural materials and local resources
- building developments that enhance rather than conflict with the environment
- careful management of scarce resources through recycling
- education on environmental issues for visitors
- effective environmental control and regulations
- minimising tourism leakage and reinvesting profits locally in projects such as education.

Build your learning

After reading the case study on Center Parcs (page 112 of the textbook), students might investigate the ways in which Oasis in the Lake District attempts to improve and preserve the natural environment. For example, Oasis has a carefully planned programme designed to protect the natural habitat of the indigenous red squirrel and protect it from threats from the grey squirrel.

Session 6

Textbook pages 118 to 123

Resources required

- OHT 2
- Club 18–30 brochures

Objectives of session

- To identify and discuss the sociocultural objectives of tourism development.

Development of textbook

- This session might be started by asking students to consider how tourism development can benefit the local community and the local culture. Ideas can be summarised using the three bullet points on page 121 of the textbook.
- The topic of promoting understanding between the culture of tourists and the host population might be explored by asking students to identify some examples of culture clashes that they might have experienced when travelling abroad.
- Students might be asked to consider the contentious issue of whose cultural habits and beliefs should take precedence, and why. For example, should they be allowed to sunbathe topless when visiting a country with strict moral codes? If they conclude that they should, they could be asked to consider the long-term effect that this might have on the host community's culture.
- When discussing the potential improvements in quality of life and increased provision of facilities, students can be asked to brainstorm examples of how this might occur. Where students live in or near a tourist destination, they might like to consider which facilities and services are only available because the area is a tourist destination.

Key words to define

Sociocultural objectives, promoting understanding, improvements to quality of life, staged authenticity, provision of community facilities.

Answers to textbook activities

Page 120: This activity can be extended by allowing students to explore and evaluate the views of the community of Goathland about the advantages and disadvantages of their village being used as the location for *Heartbeat*. For example, there seems to be some discrepancies in the statistics. Students might question why only 5 per cent of the population cites 'publicity for the area' as an advantage when this is clearly responsible for the greatest advantage cited of 'economic gain'.

Page 121: This activity will be improved if students are provided with copies of Club 18–30 holiday brochures so that they can fully appreciate the product and the extent to which the tour operator encourages potential customers to 'let your hair down'. Students who have been on a similar holiday might describe what the holiday was like. The discussion can refer back to the activity undertaken on page 116 in which students were asked to consider the reasons why many tourists do not think that tourism development damages the environment. They might discuss whether the average Club 18–30 holidaymaker would consider that their type of holiday would have any negative impact on the environment.

Build your learning

After reading the Padaung Human Zoo webstract on page 122 of the textbook, students might discuss how such a deplorable situation could arise. Their suggestions might include:

- lack of regulatory control
- little value placed on the local population – the perception that local people are simply a tourism commodity
- the desire to satisfy the perceived expectations of naive tourists by providing staged authenticity.

Session 7

Textbook pages 124 to 129

Resources required

- OHT 2
- Current information on the Millennium Dome

Objectives of session

- To identify and discuss the political objectives of tourism development.

Development of textbook

- In discussing the political objectives of tourism development, it is important that students relate their comments back to public sector tourism agents that were covered in session 2. Based on their knowledge from session 2, students might be asked to identify typical examples of political objectives. For example, they may suggest that local authorities aim to improve the image of their area or a regional tourist board might seek to establish a regional identity.
- When discussing the topic of image enhancement of an area, students might identify and discuss the different types of image that a local authority might want to create and encourage through appropriate tourism development. For example, traditional seaside resorts such as Brighton, Blackpool and Torquay have sought to attract the corporate market by developing an image of a suitable destination for conferences and exhibitions. Conversely, industrial cities such as Liverpool, Newcastle and Bradford have successfully developed an image of being a cosmopolitan short-break tourist destination.
- When discussing the political objective of creating a regional or national identity, you might like to use the example of 'Cool Britannia', see page 245 of the textbook. Students could be asked to identify areas of the UK that they consider as having a clear regional identity. Examples might include the Lake District.

Key words to define

Political objectives, image enhancement, regional identity, national identity.

Answers to textbook activities

Page 129: Issues surrounding the development and management of the Millennium Dome have changed dramatically since the textbook was printed and students will need to be aware of its current status. You might provide newspaper reports to ensure that students are up-to-date with developments. However, students can use the information in the case study to complete the activity.

It is useful to link the discussion on the Millennium Dome to the marketing unit, using it to illustrate the difference between a product-led approach to marketing as opposed to a customer-led approach. For example, students might consider the extent to which the entire Dome concept was vague at the product development stage and, arguably, not based on identified and measurable customer needs.

Build your learning

In preparation for the next three sessions students should review the content of the last four sessions that have covered the objectives of tourism developments. They could be asked to outline what they consider to be the main positive and negative impacts of tourism development.

Session 8

Textbook pages 130 to 133

Resources required

- OHT 3

Objectives of session

- To identify and discuss the economic impacts of tourism development.

Development of textbook

- If students have undertaken the build your learning activity suggested at the end of session 7, they should be asked to brainstorm the main positive and negative impacts of tourism development. Students' suggestions can be summarised using OHT 3.

- Students should be able to define the term infrastructure and identify all of its components. You might refer back to the Zenith case study (page 105 of the textbook) and the concern that the road system and water supply might not be able to cope with the influx of tourists attracted to the new development. The potential impact on the infrastructure could be either positive or negative. For example, if nothing is done to improve the road system it could result in heavy traffic congestion – a negative impact. However, if the road system is improved it could have positive benefits for both visitors and the host population.
- The topics of the loss of traditional employment opportunities and the increased cost of living might be related back to the discussions in session 1 on landowners and session 2 on farm tourism. Students might consider the effect on jobs and cost of living when farmers convert land to tourism development.

Key words to define

Positive effects of tourism, negative effects of tourism, economic impacts, improvements in the infrastructure, loss of traditional employment opportunities, increase in the cost of living.

Answers to textbook activities

Page 132: The first part of this activity can be linked to the marketing unit and the topic of public relations. It can also provide evidence for key skills in communication.

Page 133: Students can link this activity to other negative impacts of tourism development. For example, a migration of young adults will often result in a skills shortage in the local workforce and the subsequent loss of traditional jobs. There may be some erosion of local cultural values with the influx of outsiders and an exodus of local people. A further issue that students might consider is the effect that occasional visitors (such as second homeowners that probably only visit at certain times of the year) may have on the local economy. For example, a permanent population might provide sufficient custom to sustain small local shops, however infrequent visitors may not provide enough custom on a regular basis.

Build your learning

Tutors might provide students with the main headings from Figure 2.5 (page 130 of the textbook) and ask them to discuss and fill in the main 'pros' and 'cons' for each heading.

Session 9

Textbook pages 133–135

Resources required

- OHT 3
- Access to the internet

Objectives of session

- To identify and discuss the environmental impacts of tourism development.

Development of textbook

- This session can be introduced by using OHT 3 to remind students of the impacts that tourism development can have. Students can then be asked to brainstorm the environmental impacts that tourism development can have.
- Students should explore the meaning of the term pollution and understand that it does not simply mean litter but includes noise, engine exhausts, fumes, etc.
- When looking at the environmental impacts of overcrowding and increased wear and tear, students might consider examples such as the Lake District. They should understand that even when visitors take a responsible attitude towards the environment, and attempt to behave in a way that will not have negative impacts, problems can still arise. For example, large numbers of visitors walking along country footpaths will cause erosion.

- You might ask students to consider the development of out-of-town shopping centres and the extent to which this may reduce environmental impact on neighbouring areas. Does channelling large numbers of visitors into a shopping mall prevent congestion and overcrowding in neighbouring towns and cities? Or does it simply shift the negative environmental impacts to another area, since the construction of the malls and the necessary transport links inevitably dominate the landscape and local environment?

Key words to define

Environmental impacts, pollution, overcrowding, traffic congestion, increased wear and tear, inappropriate development, conflicts with host community.

Answers to textbook activities

Page 135: Students might identify some of the advantages as income generation, job creation and planned preservation of the area as a national park. Some of the disadvantages are that employment is seasonal, there is a threat to traditional farming jobs, increased traffic congestion and pollution, high local housing costs, erosion of footpaths and bridleways and conflict between cyclists and walkers. When undertaking the second part of the activity students gain evidence for key skills in communication.

Build your learning

In preparation for the next session students can be asked to identify some of the sociocultural impacts of tourism development. It is important that they investigate international issues rather than confining their research to local or UK issues. They might visit the VSO (www. vso.org,uk) or Tourism Concern (www. tourismconcern.org.uk) websites for their research. You might ask each student to come to the next session with information based on research on a different overseas country.

Session 10

Textbook pages 136 to 142

Resources required

- OHT 3
- Package holiday brochures featuring Dominican Republic and Slovenia
- Access to a library or learning resource centre with geography and history books
- Access to the internet

Objectives of session

- To identify and discuss the sociocultural impacts of tourism development.

Development of textbook

- This session can be started by using OHT 3 to recap on the three main types of tourism development impact. If students undertook the 'build your learning' activity in session 9, they can give a brief report of their main findings to the rest of the group. The group can discuss the various issues raised and list key concerns on the whiteboard.
- Students should understand that tourism development can, and often does, have positive sociocultural impacts. You might illustrate this using the Sinai eco-resort case study (pages 117–8 of the textbook).
- Students might consider and discuss the extent to which the scale of tourism development can affect the degree of sociocultural impact. For example, where an entire country such as Dominican Republic is rapidly developed into a tourist destination the sociocultural impact is likely to be far greater than when development is limited to small areas. In the latter case, there is a far greater chance of local sociocultural values being retained and unaffected by visitors.
- Using the case study on pages 136–7 of the textbook, students might debate the moral and ethical issues involved in sex tourism. For example, if the women involved in prostitution argue that the trade provides a higher standard of living for themselves and their families does this justify the sex tourism industry? Students should understand that this is a highly complex issue with no simple solutions.

Key words to define

Sociocultural impact.

Answers to textbook activities

Page 137: Students might present their findings from this activity in the form of a table. In the left column, they can list the traditional sociocultural values; and in the right column, identify any possible conflicts that tourism development might cause. For example, the traditional sociocultural value of strict religious beliefs might conflict with the more promiscuous attitude of tourists.

Page 142: In preparation for the external unit assessment it is suggested that students present this activity as a written report. You might like to provide students with an outline as to how the report should be presented:

- introduction, to include a brief overview of the development of the Gambia as a tourist destination
- positive and negative economic impacts
- positive and negative environmental impacts
- positive and negative sociocultural impacts
- summary and conclusion.

Build your learning

Using the case studies and other information that they may have researched, students might discuss how the impacts of tourism development in the Gambia are echoed in other countries. They may suggest ways in which other countries have avoided some of the negative impacts that have occurred in the Gambia.

Session 11

Textbook pages 143 to 146

Resources required

- OHT 4

Objectives of session

- To identify and discuss how the positive impacts of tourism development can be maximised.

Development of textbook

- Based on their learning from the first 10 sessions of this unit, students should be asked to identify some of the ways in which responsible tourism developers can maximise the positive impacts of tourism. Ideas can be listed on the whiteboard and consolidated using OHT 4.
- When discussing the topic of the retention of visitor spending, you should remind students of previous discussions on tourism leakage. Students should be able to distinguish between the retention of spending within an area and retention within a specific development. For example, an all-inclusive holiday resort may retain its guest's spending within the hotel complex; the spending rarely benefits the local community.
- The topic of the investment of tourism income can be linked to the marketing unit and public relations activity. Many private sector providers donate some of their profits in the form of community grants and sponsorship to improve their public image.
- Students should discuss the difference between tourism providing increased job opportunities and providing training and development for specific tourism jobs. For example, in countries such as the Gambia, tourism development may provide jobs for the local population but these tend to be manual, unskilled or semi-skilled and low paid. The more skilled jobs tend to be filled by overseas personnel employed by international operators. Clearly, to maximise the positive impacts, it would be preferable to train and develop local people to take on higher paid and more skilled jobs.

SESSION PLANS

Key words to define

Maximising positive impacts, retention of visitor spending, investing tourism income, widening access, staff training and development, training and employment of local people, tourism education.

Answers to textbook activities

Page 145: For this activity you might arrange for a guest speaker from a local travel or tourism organisation to talk to students about the types of training and staff development that their organisation carries out.

Page 146: Students might identify that h, d and e are positive actions that could have a profound effect; f, b, and e are less effective actions as there is no way of knowing whether or not the money and gifts will benefit the local population; and action a is of little use.

Build your learning

In preparation for the next session students can be asked to consider how the negative impacts of tourism can be minimised through responsible tourism development.

Session 12

Textbook pages 147 to 150

Resources required

- OHT 5
- Holiday brochures that include the mass market destinations similar to Benidorm such as Torremelinos, Magaluf, San Antonia, etc.
- Old photographs of the local area such as the main shopping area

Objectives of session

- To identify and discuss how the negative impacts of tourism development can be minimised through planning control and the principles of sustainable tourism.

Development of textbook

- Start by asking students to suggest ways in which the negative impacts of tourism can be minimised. Ideas can be listed on the whiteboard and consolidated using OHT 5.
- In discussing the topic of planning permission, students should be aware that it does not simply relate to the construction of a new building but also covers change of use, alterations to a building, frontage, signage, etc. They should understand that consideration of planning permission applications involves a wide range of issues. For example, it may appear justified for a farmer to apply to convert existing farmland to a golf course on the basis that the landscape will remain relatively unchanged. However, negative impacts might be the loss of farming land and traditional farming job opportunities.
- You will need to explain fully the term sustainable tourism. Students can be asked to suggest examples of sustainability. Students can discuss what they think is meant by each of the twelve bullet points listed in the British government's 'A Better Quality of Life' initiative (see page 148 of the textbook). For example, what does 'putting people at the centre' mean? Who are the people – the host population, tourism development agents, visitors or all three?

Key words to define

Minimising negative impact, planning control, ecotourism, sustainable tourism, Agenda 21.

Answers to textbook activities

Page 150: As an alternative to this activity, you might like to arrange a group visit. With permission, students could visit an area that has recently been regenerated and developed and evaluate the extent to which the development has been based on sustainable principles. They might discuss the extent to which

the original character and history of the area has been preserved for future generations.

Where old photographs are available of the local area these can also provide a useful basis for discussion on sustainability. Photographs of shopping areas are particularly good as they are likely to show substantial changes. Even if the actual buildings remain unchanged, students should notice the way in which shop frontages and signage can change the character of an area.

Build your learning

After reading the Benidorm case study (page 149 of the textbook), students can use holiday brochures that feature resorts that underwent a similar rapid development and influx of visitors as Benidorm. They should read the brochure descriptions of each resort and identify any evidence that the principles of sustainability have been applied to the resort development.

Session 13

Textbook pages 150 to 151

Resources required

- OHT 5
- Road map of a town centre that currently allows vehicular access to all areas

Objectives of session

- To identify and discuss how the negative impacts of tourism development can be minimised through visitor and traffic management.

Development of textbook

- The session can be introduced by using OHT 5 to recap on the main ways in which the negative impacts of tourism development can be minimised.
- Students should be aware of the possible conflicts that arise from tourist development and attempting to minimise the negative impact of traffic and visitors. For example, although heavy traffic congestion is clearly undesirable, tourism agents cannot afford to discourage visitors by placing prohibitive restrictions on transport that make access to tourism destinations difficult. In effect, you cannot say 'we don't want visitor traffic but we want visitors'. Students might then suggest ways in which traffic congestion might be minimised without reducing the level of access for visitors. Their discussions can be consolidated using the four bullet points on page 150 of the textbook.
- Working in small groups by using a town road map, ask students to suggest ways in which traffic could be kept out of the centre. They may suggest suitable locations for car parks and park and ride services. They should also consider access for different types of visitors, such as coach parties, hotel guests with luggage and disabled badge holders.
- The topic of destination management will need to be explained to students. Where possible it is useful for students to see such a system in operation. Tutors may be able to arrange for students to visit a local tourist information centre and evaluate how the centre uses destination management.

Key words to define

Visitor management, traffic management, destination management systems.

Answers to textbook activities

Page 151: This activity can be extended by asking students to carry out a survey of visitors who have travelled to the area by car. Students might ask questions such as:

- how easy it was to get to the town – was there any traffic congestion
- where the visitor has parked
- how easy it was to find parking
- how effective is the directional signage in the town?

This activity can be linked to the unit on customer service in terms of meeting customer needs and providing information and the marketing unit in terms of conducting face-to-face primary research. Students can also gather evidence for key skills in communication and IT and application of number if they analyse their findings numerically and present them in graphical format.

Build your learning

Most local newspapers carry frequent coverage of traffic issues and concerns in the form of both editorial and readers' letters. Students can use these papers to identify some of the main local issues. For example, what concerns are there over local 'black spots' and congested areas? What suggestions, if any, have been made to tackle these problems?

Session 14

Textbook pages 151 to 155

Resources required

- OHT 6

Objectives of session

- To identify and discuss how the negative impacts of tourism development can be minimised through environmental impact assessments and environmental audits.

Development of textbook

- Although students are not likely to have an in-depth knowledge of how environmental impact assessments and environmental audits operate, it is important that they understand how and why organisations use them.
- Students should understand that environmental impact assessments are closely linked to the principles of sustainable tourism. Responsible tourism development agents carry out these assessments before developing a tourism product or service to ensure that it will comply with sustainable principles. Students should be asked to consider what they think might be assessed in an environmental impact assessment. You can consolidate the suggestions using the five bullet points on page 151 of the textbook.
- You might illustrate how each of the points could be applied by using the case study on the Zenith project on page 105 of the textbook. For example, the negative impacts that might be identified as needing to be minimised could be the increase in traffic and the extra burden placed on the infrastructure.
- When discussing the topic of environmental auditing, tutors might provide students with the definition on page 152 of the textbook and ask students to consider what is meant by 'key activities'. Students should be aware that key activities encompass an extensive range of activities. For example, when a hotel provides a guest with accommodation this involves a number of activities – such as laundry, cleaning, provisions, power, etc. – which can have potential negative impacts. Using OHT 6, tutors should explain the steps involved in carrying out an environmental audit.

Key words to define

Environmental impact assessment, environmental audit.

Answers to textbook activities

Page 153: This activity would be particularly useful to students if combined with a visit to a fast food restaurant or with a talk from a representative of a fast food organisation. Many fast food chains have developed responsible policies regarding packaging and litter disposal; for example, many restaurant chains use recyclable materials and ensure that staff regularly clean up any litter discarded outside the premises.

Students might also undertake an evaluation of a range of takeaways in their area and identify which are responsible for the greatest amount of discarded packaging on the streets.

Build your learning

In preparation for the next session students should read through all their class notes together with any information that they have collected and ensure that they fully understand all aspects of tourism development.

Session 15

Resources required

- Sample external assessment/s from the awarding body
- OHTs 1-6.
- List of 'key words to define' from sessions 1–14

Objectives of session

- To prepare for the external unit assessment.

Development of textbook

- This session might be started by revisiting all the 'key words to define' from each of the last 14 sessions. You could write the words on separate slips of paper and create a team competition with each team scoring points for giving a correct definition. You may then recap on the key topics by going through OHTs 1–6.
- The remainder of the session should be spent using the sample external assessment materials and guidance provided by the awarding body. Where the external assessment is based on pre-seen case study material, students should evaluate the material using all of the topics listed in the specification's 'What you need to learn' section.
- You may decide that a number of sessions need to be arranged for students' preparation for external assessment.

Tourism development agents

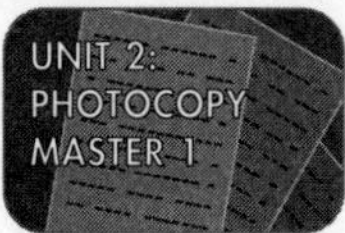

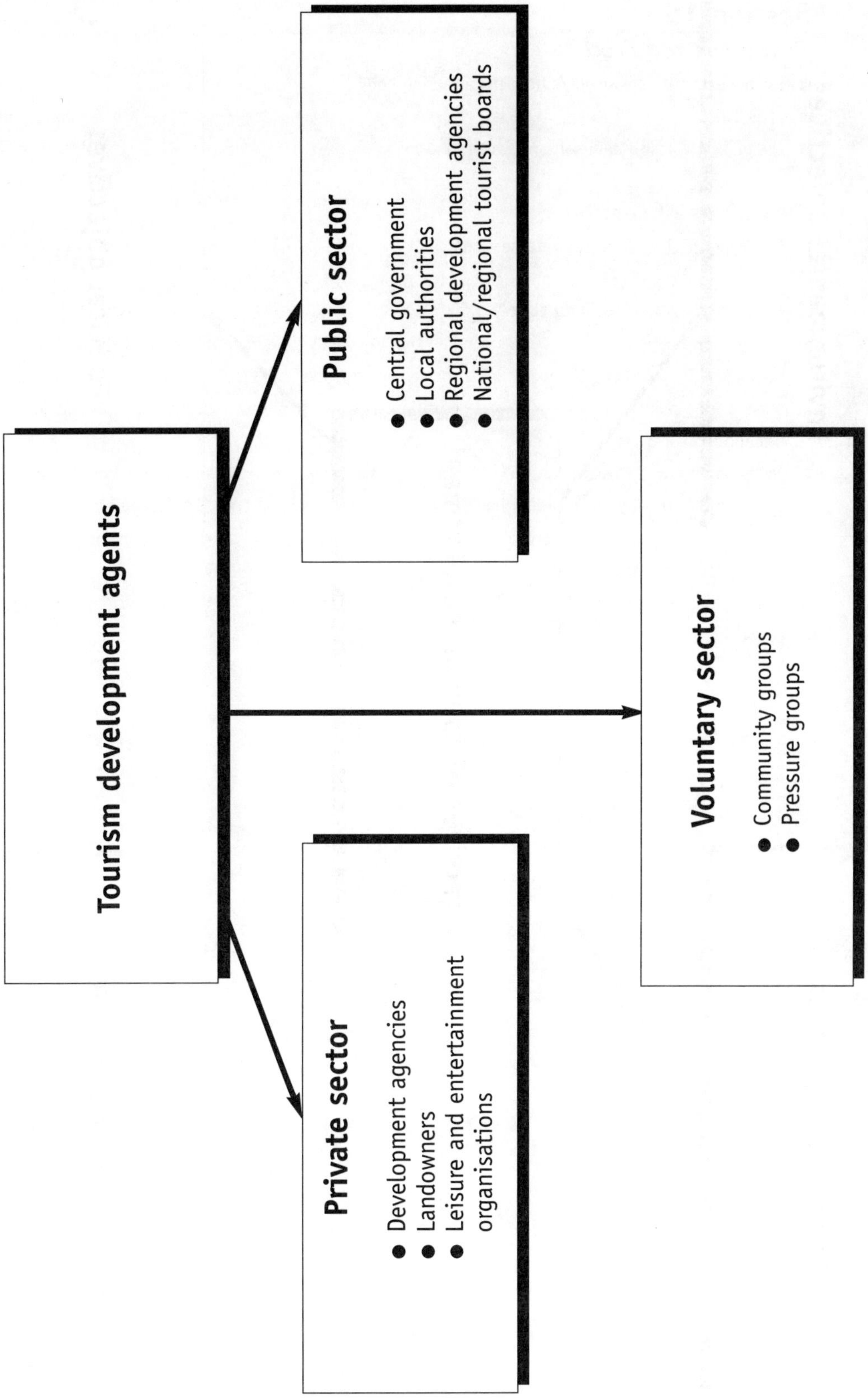

UNIT 2: PHOTOCOPY MASTER 1

Tourism development agents
Public sector
● Central government
● Local authorities
● Regional development agencies
● National/regional tourist boards
Voluntary sector
● Community groups
● Pressure groups
Private sector
● Development agencies
● Landowners
● Leisure and entertainment organisations

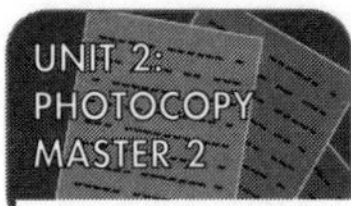

Objectives of tourism development

Environmental objectives

Political objectives

Objectives of tourism development

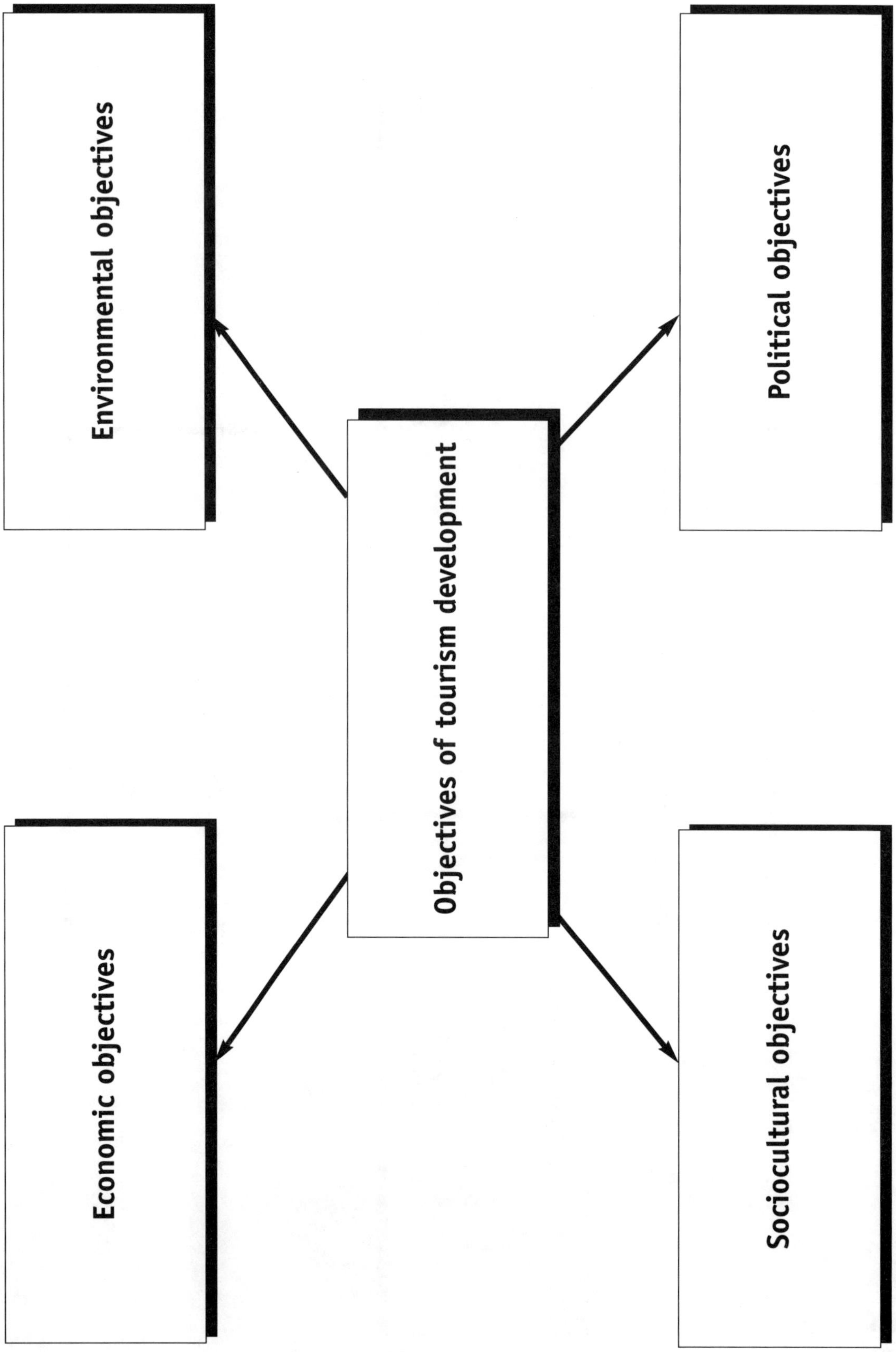

Economic objectives

Sociocultural objectives

Impacts of tourism development

UNIT 2: PHOTOCOPY MASTER 3

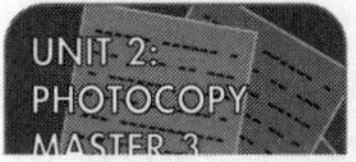

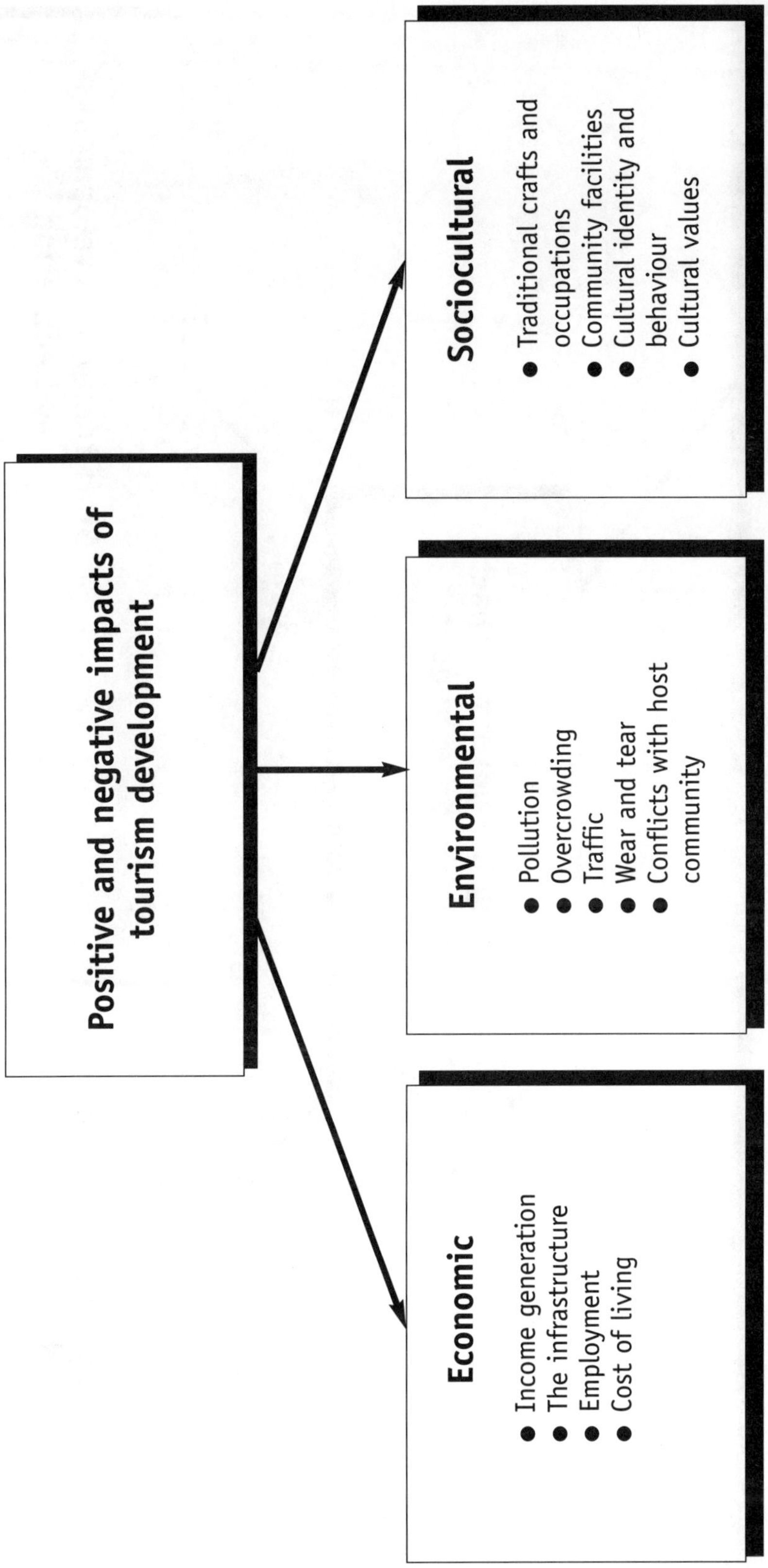

Positive and negative impacts of tourism development
Economic
● Income generation
● The infrastructure
● Employment
● Cost of living
Environmental
● Pollution
● Overcrowding
● Traffic
● Wear and tear
● Conflicts with host community
Sociocultural
● Traditional crafts and occupations
● Community facilities
● Cultural identity and behaviour
● Cultural values

UNIT 2: PHOTOCOPY MASTER 4

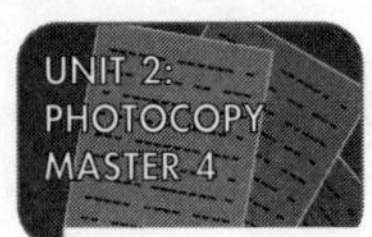

Maximising positive impacts

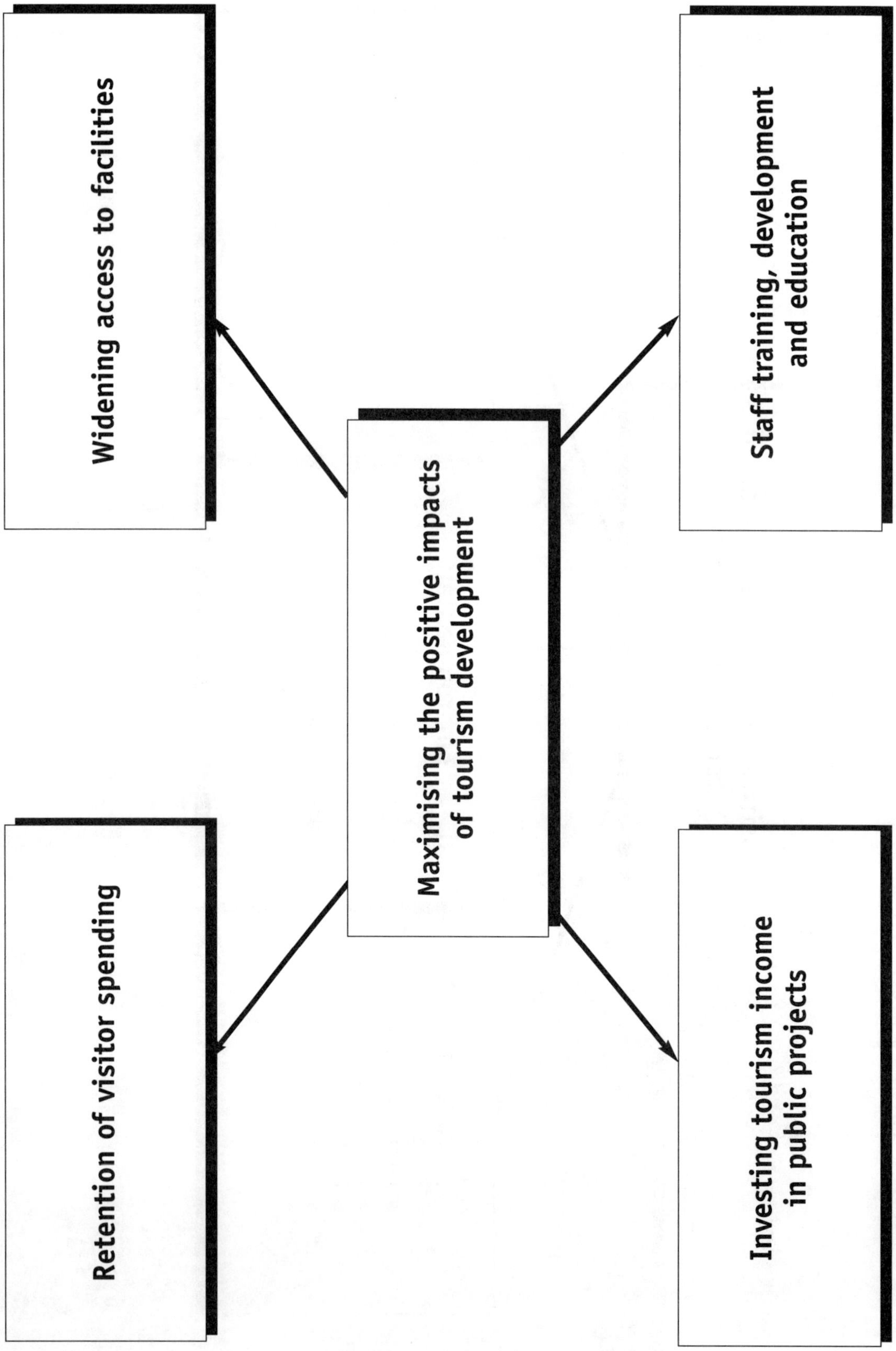
Maximising the positive impacts of tourism development
Widening access to facilities
Staff training, development and education
Retention of visitor spending
Investing tourism income in public projects

Minimising negative impacts

UNIT 2: PHOTOCOPY MASTER 5

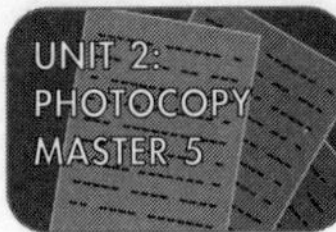

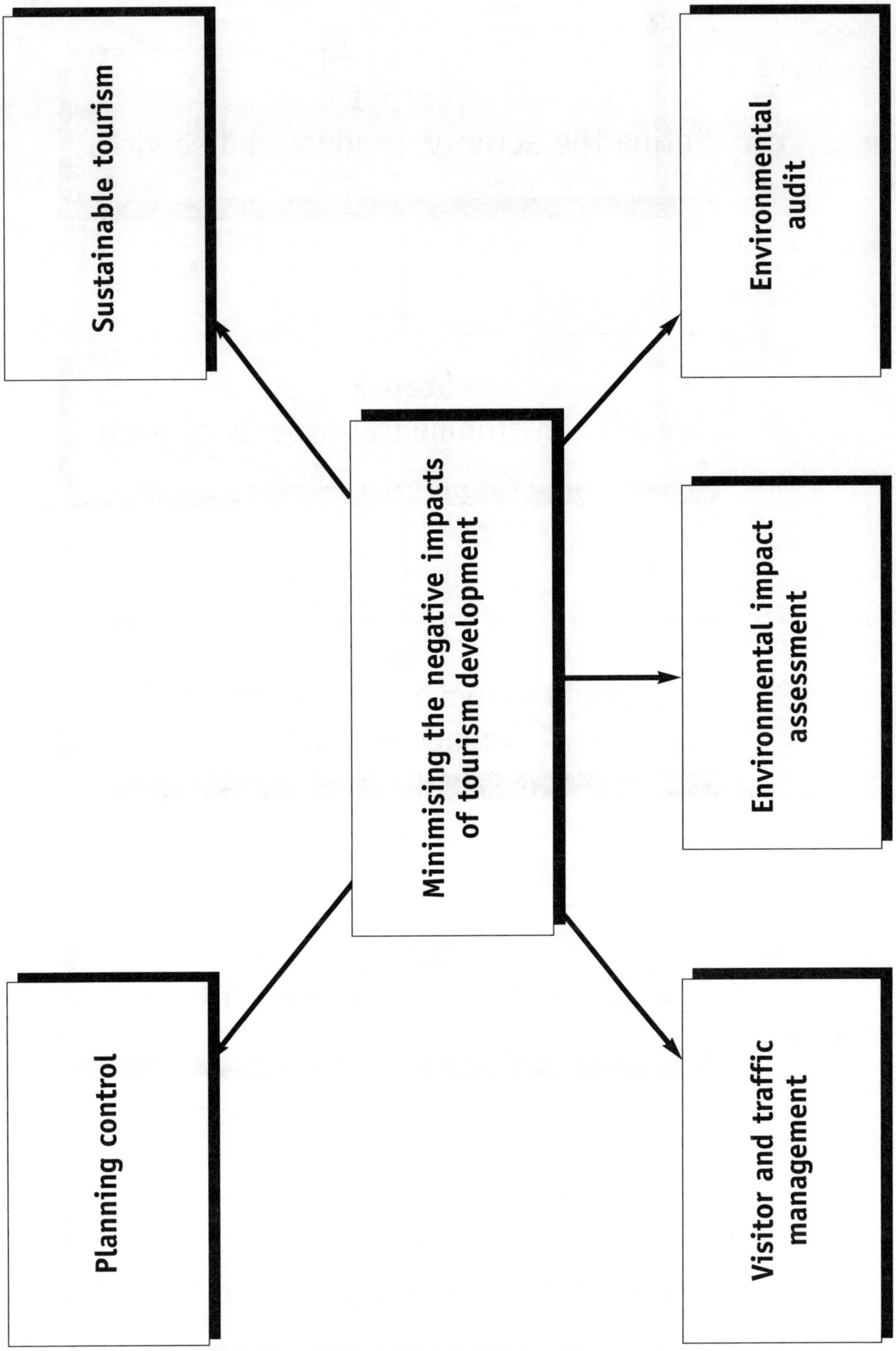

Minimising the negative impacts of tourism development
Sustainable tourism
Environmental audit
Environmental impact assessment
Planning control
Visitor and traffic management

UNIT 2: PHOTOCOPY MASTER 6

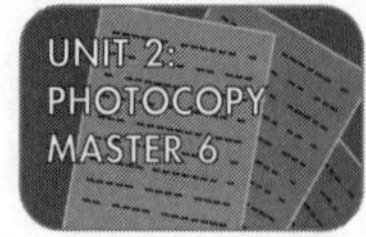

Conducting an environmental impact

Environmental audit

Step 1
Define the activity, product and services

↓

Step 2
Identify environmental aspects of each

↓

Step 3
Identify associated environmental impact of each

↓

Step 4
Determine significance of each impact

↓

Step 5
Draw up a register of aspects and impacts

Unit 3:
Worldwide travel destinations

Introduction

This unit introduces the main worldwide travel destinations popular with UK tourists. It aims to provide students with the opportunity to improve their knowledge of the major continental European and long-haul destinations and to assess the attraction and key features of these resorts.

Delivery suggestions

Employers often expect sound knowledge of the main worldwide travel destinations and the means to research and report on new and developing resorts. Students also need to be aware of the different types of tourist destination, characteristics, gateways, routes and popularity (pages 158–202) before embarking on their individual case studies. This unit is a useful way to introduce various sources of information and methods of research.

Students will require source material. Guide books, brochures, leaflets, country information, atlases, visitor information and the internet will be in demand. It would be useful to ask travel agents if they can supply old editions of publications that may assist students with their research. If students choose their case studies early enough, then they may be able to obtain useful information from the appropriate national tourist office. It would be wise to coordinate this effort, so that not everyone writes to the same organisation asking for similar material.

Unit planner

Session	Session objectives	Text pages
1	To introduce the topic of worldwide travel destinations, making the distinction between short-haul and long-haul destinations To identify the leading destinations for UK tourists	158 to 162
2	To identify different types of tourist destination: (a) towns and cities and (b) seaside resorts	163 to 168
3	To identify different types of tourist destination: (c) purpose-built resorts, (d) countryside areas and (e) historic destinations	169 to 173
4	To explain the characteristics of tourist destinations: (a) climate and (b) natural attractions	174 to 178
5	To explain the characteristics of tourist destinations: (c) built attractions, (d) events and (e) entertainment	178 to 181
6	To explain the characteristics of tourist destinations: (f) accommodation types, (g) transport and (h) access	181 to 183
7	To identify the main travel and tourism gateways	184 to 186
8	To identify the main travel routes that tourists use when travelling to their holiday destinations	186 to 191
9	To explain the fluctuating popularity of tourist destinations caused by: (a) economic factors	192 to 193
10	To explain the fluctuating popularity of tourist destinations caused by: (b) social and political factors	194 to 199
11	To explain the fluctuating popularity of tourist destinations caused by: (c) geographical and environmental factors To identify the main transport principals serving a destination	199 to 202
12 and 13	To produce assessment evidence for the unit To investigate and examine two short-haul destinations, examples include Spain and France	203 to 210
14 and 15	To produce assessment evidence for the unit To investigate and examine long-haul destinations, choosing two from North America, the Caribbean and Australasia	211 to 215

Session 1

Textbook pages 158 to 162

Resources required

- Atlases
- Calculators
- Blank world outline maps

Objectives of session

- To introduce the topic of worldwide travel destinations, making the distinction between short-haul and long-haul destinations.
- To identify the leading destinations for UK tourists.

Development of textbook

- Asking students where they have been on holiday is a good way of introducing worldwide travel destinations. These can then be categorised as short-haul or long-haul destinations; students should be aware of these terms, which are covered in Unit 1 (page 5). The list of destinations produced by students can also be categorised in terms of the five types of tourism destinations from page 158.
- Students need to be aware of which areas, cities and resorts are the most popular short-haul and long-haul destinations. Compare the list of destinations suggested by students with the data in the activity on page 160 and Figure 3.2 on page 161. Students can be asked the reasons why they chose a particular holiday destination.
- The session may be concluded by briefly explaining the format of the external assessment for this unit. Students should be advised that once they have an idea on what area they would like to research, then any information relating to those destinations should be kept in the student's folder until it is required.

Key words to define

Travel destination, tourism destination, short-haul destination, long-haul destination, traffic conference areas, the Commonwealth.

Answers to textbook activities

Page 159: Students can list the countries according to the correct zone or plot them on a world map. If students are listing them, they need to make the distinction between short-haul and long-haul in zone 2. In task 3 Mr and Mrs Mitchell, Ramesh, Jasmine, and Ruth and Harry are undertaking long-haul journeys; Mr White, John, Mrs Madhani and Enasha are short-haul passengers.

Page 160: Reasons include that France and Spain are geographically close to the UK; many Spanish package holidays are promoted; France is easily accessible via ferry and Channel Tunnel services.

The percentage change in visitor numbers is Spain +66%, France +31%, United States +31%, Greece –7%, Italy +54%, Portugal +4%, Turkey +3%, Cyprus, Malta, Gibraltar –17%, Republic of Ireland +60%, The Netherlands +4%, Belgium +33%, Germany –12%, Eastern Europe –8%, Other short-haul +12%, Long-haul +90%, Total +38%.

The countries that have seen the most rapid increase in visitor numbers are:

- Spain – increase in cheaper flights, growth in the popularity of package holidays, development of resorts such as Ibiza, value of the pound
- Republic of Ireland – IRA ceasefire and peace treaty, popular television programmes such as Father Ted and Ballykissangel promoting Irish interest, Irish pubs, beer and music
- Italy – greater varieties of Italian food and wine consumed by the British public, value of the pound, promotion of Italian football, increase in cheaper flights, the arts (famous artists and galleries).

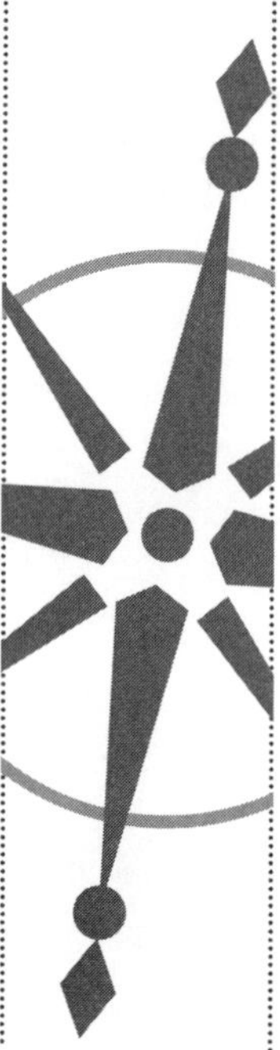

Build your learning

Students should be able to identify those countries which have shown a marked increase and those which have shown a decline, quoting figures from the Figure 3.2. A distinction should be made between the percentage change in 1996–98, the percentage of tourist numbers and the actual number of tourists.

Throughout the following sessions, students should consider which countries they would like to study for the assessment in sessions 12–15. This is important so that they can begin to collect information and to contact the appropriate national tourist offices (NTOs) if required. Students should be encouraged to provide a stamped addressed reply envelope and give clear details of what they require from NTOs. Students should not expect the NTOs to research the assessments and activities on their behalf.

Session 2

Textbook pages 163 to 168

Resources required

Summer or winter sun holiday brochures

Objectives of session

- To identify different types of tourist destination:
  (a) towns and cities
  (b) seaside resorts.

Development of textbook

- This session should start by introducing the five main types of tourist destination. This can be introduced by a brainstorm activity with students giving examples of each of the five types of tourist destination: towns and cities, seaside resorts, purpose-built resorts, countryside areas, and historical and cultural destinations.
- Each student could choose a city destination and use the headings on pages 163 to 164 to examine reasons why different people may choose to visit the selected city. Brochures, guide books and the internet provide a wide variety of information.
- The reasons for the location of popular short-haul beach resort destinations could be explored using Figure 3.5. It is important for students to be aware of the geographical location of the main resorts and the reasons why many are located on the Mediterranean.

Key words to define

Towns and cities, beach boredom.

Answers to textbook activities

Page 163: All the cities are short-haul destinations apart from New York. The cities that increased in popularity between 1998 and 1999 are Rome, Venice, Madrid, Lille, New York and Seville. The top four destinations – Paris, Amsterdam, Bruges and Brussels – are geographically close to the UK, have good access and offer regular connecting services.

Page 165: Reasons include that the Channel Tunnel has made travel easier, travel is cheaper, and the growth of European, American and Asian markets. For task 2, students usually suggest main cities. Short-haul destinations will be similar to those listed in Figure 3.3. Benefits for towns and cities of conference and exhibition business include income generation, prestige, employment opportunities, improved infrastructure, further investment by companies seeking to capitalise on growth, increased range of services and opportunities for businesses in the host country.

Page 166: Students can work in small groups for this activity and present their ideas to the rest of the group. Holiday brochures are useful to explore the range of features in each of the two beach resorts.

Strengths and weaknesses can be based on the level of provision and range of activities on offer at each of the resorts. For task 2, the main types of customers can be identified by looking at brochure photographs and focusing on the intended client group by the advertised range of activities and services being offered. For task 3, peak seasons can be identified through pricing structures and through official statistics.

Build your learning

Using the extract on page 168, students may wish to explore the range of activities on offer and note which destinations have the greatest and the fewest choices. They can then consider if this has a bearing on the size or popularity of the resort. Further consideration may be made to the way in which the information is presented and what has been left out by the table. Attention should be given to the lack of information on the level of provision or the quality of the service.

Session 3

Textbook pages 169 to 173

Resources required

Brochures and guide books on purpose-built resorts, theme parks, skiing and historical and cultural destinations

Objectives of session

- To identify different types of tourist destination:
  (c) purpose-built resorts
  (d) countryside areas
  (e) historic destinations.

Development of textbook

- This session links with the previous session and reference should be made to the five main types of tourist destinations. Examples should be given from both short-haul and long-haul destinations rather than those in the UK.
- Using Figure 3.6 (on page 170 of the textbook), students might discuss the attraction of the countryside as a popular tourist destination. Students may wish to select a brochure that includes one of these areas and discover how it is being marketed to its target audience. You can conclude by outlining the range of possible activities from walking to outdoor pursuits and adventure holidays.
- In terms of defining heritage tourism, students may suggest a range of examples possibly from the UK but would need to add short-haul and long-haul examples as well. The term culture is not synonymous with historic, and you might suggest a range of countries that offer different cultural (as opposed to historic) experiences. The list is a useful starting point to considering similarities and differences between cultures.

Key words to define

Purpose-built resorts, countryside areas, historic and cultural destinations, heritage tourism, culture.

Answers to textbook activities

Page 169 'Purpose-built resorts': Students could be placed into groups allowing the comparison of different purpose-built resorts to take place. Brochures may be supplemented by information gleaned from the internet. Different client groups may be reflected in the use of photographs within the brochure, written statements or range of suggested activities.

Page 169 'Theme park resorts': Again the internet may be a useful way of supplementing information obtained from brochures. Give students different theme parks to research, and then allow them to make comparisons between European, or short-haul, theme parks, and American, or long-haul, theme parks. The list of facilities and attractions should not just be limited to various rides but also consider

accommodation, hospitality, retail and the needs of customers. Describing why the theme park resort is popular with UK tourists should move beyond the various rides to incorporate theme park design, the overall theme or concept, location, climate, access and price.

Page 171: The location of various short-haul and long-haul ski resorts can be mapped. Clusters of resorts can then be identified. Brochures are necessary for this activity.

Page 172: Students should avoid using UK examples in this activity. Many guide books, brochures and websites can supply information. Students should avoid presenting a history of their chosen destinations.

Build your learning

Students could provide two examples of each of the five types of tourist destination. Brochures and guidebooks are essential for this activity, and the information may be presented on an annotated map. The second part of the end of section activity serves as a case study.

Session 4

Textbook pages 174 to 178

Resources required

- Calculators
- Holiday brochures
- Atlases
- Access to the internet

Objectives of session

- To explain the characteristics of tourist destinations:
  (a) climate
  (b) natural attractions.

Development of textbook

- The session starts to look at the particular features of each of the five destination types. It begins by looking at climate, and students should move beyond describing destinations as simply hot or cold. Climate information can be summarised in a table for easy reference.
- Using a number of climate graphs, students can compare a variety of different destinations. If climate data is available then students can draw their own climate graph. Climate graphs may be found in atlases, travel guides and holiday brochures. The World Travel Guide has a selection of climate graphs which can be accessed at www.worldtravelguide.net.
- A brainstorm activity is a good way of getting students to think of a range of natural attractions. Types of natural attractions, with examples, can be listed. Holiday brochures could also be used to identify a range of holiday destinations that incorporate a natural attraction. Students may consider how natural attractions are modified for the purposes of tourism or are affected by the actions of tourists.

Key words to define

Climate zones, climate graphs, topography.

Answers to textbook activities

Page 176: The warmest month is July with an average temperature of 21°C. The temperature range is 21°C – 9°C = 12°C (measurements taken from the middle of the month against the temperature line on the climate graph). The wettest month of the year is November with 170 mm of rainfall. Climate graphs are found in most holiday brochures and in some atlases. Appeal of climate should be linked to the intended activity of the tourists. For example, a beach holiday should experience minimum rainfall and warm temperatures; a skiing holiday requires different climatic conditions.

Page 177: Average daily maximum temperature in the UK is April 13˚C, May 15.8˚C, June 19.5˚C, July 21.5˚C, August 21˚C, September 18.5˚C, October 13˚C. Average daily maximum temperature in Ibiza is April 19.5˚C, May 22.7˚C, June 26˚C, July 29.3˚C, August 29.3˚C, September 22.7˚C.

Sunshine figures are based on daily averages. Students need to know how many days there are in the month to calculate hours of sunshine between April and October. The UK hours of sunshine between April and October is 1,161 (5 x 30 + 6 x 31 + 7 x 30 + 6 x 31 + 6 x 31 + 5 x 30 + 3 x 31). The average daily sunshine is 5.43 hours – 1,161 hours of sunshine (divided by) 214 days. Ibiza has 1,928 hours of sunshine, which equates to 9.01 average daily hours of sunshine. Ibiza, on average, has 767 more hours of sunshine from April to October compared to the UK.

Maximum average temperatures give an idea on likely temperatures to be experienced, help to promote destinations as warm and therefore attractive locations.

The popular months for UK tourists to Ibiza are July and August. These are the hottest months, with average temperatures of 84˚F and 11 daily hours of sunshine.

Page 178: Countries with most Blue Flag awards are Spain 329, Greece 311, France 271 and Italy 219. The UK has only 59 awards. Cleanliness is attractive, safe, clean, free of pollution, beautiful, managed, inspected and regulated. Logos used to help promote beaches and inform people that a beach is clean.

Build your learning

Students may research the criteria for the Blue Flag awards, which are awarded by the Keep Britain Tidy Group in the UK. The criteria is based on European standards and can be viewed at www.tidybritain.org.uk/psea.htm. Students should ignore the Seaside Awards which are solely UK based. Students may draw up a table of natural attractions from both long-haul and short-haul destinations and also from different climatic zones.

Session 5

Textbook pages 178 to 181

Resources required

- Holiday brochures
- Travel guides
- Event listings
- Access to the internet

Objectives of session

- To explain the characteristics of tourist destinations:
  (c) built attractions
  (d) events
  (e) entertainment.

Development of textbook

- Pictures of popular built attractions such as the Eiffel Tower could be presented to the class. Ask students to identify the feature and the correct location or country. Built attractions are designed for different purposes and these can be explored using a variety of images. Students could also add to the examples on pages 178 to 179 by researching historical buildings, monuments, churches, stately homes, theme parks, museums and art galleries.
- Students can usually offer examples of events, such as music festivals. These should be explored using descriptions of location, time of year and a list of main attractions. For comparison, you could introduce other events such as the Edinburgh Festival and sporting and cultural events. Get students to consider why events happen and why large numbers of people attend them. Students should be made aware that various events are suited to different groups of people. Present a list of people of various ages and backgrounds and get students to suggest suitable events that they might wish to attend.

- Different types of entertainment should be discussed, with examples of where and when they will be found. Again, the chosen entertainment can be assessed against the potential client group or type of tourist. This leads into the activity on page 181.
- The Kitty O'Shea picture on page 181 could be used as the starting point for a discussion. Ask students why Irish theme pubs and bars are popular outside of Ireland. Are there any other examples of this type of phenomenon, for example TGI Fridays, Chiquitos, Frankie and Bennies, etc. Questions about authenticity and accurate representation of cultures could be explored here.
- Consider the timing of events and entertainment in different countries. Students can be given a country or destination to research and find out what events are happening. Students could be given a brief to find events and entertainment suitable for children, teenagers, adults and retired people. Entertainment should extend to suitable restaurants, bars and nightlife. Time Out contains listings for international events which can be found at www.timeout.com.

Key words to define

Built attractions, chateaux, events, cuisine, bars and restaurants.

Answers to textbook activities

Page 180: Students can be given different countries to research so that they can exchange information in the form of a presentation or handout. The type of tourist should be described in terms of likely age group, gender, interests, background, etc.

Page 181: This activity is best achieved after types of variables have been discussed. The type of tourist should be described in terms of age, accompanying children, income and any other agreed variables. Students should avoid the use of simple categories such as old and young. To extend this activity, examples from holiday brochures could be used. It is good practice to quote real examples where possible.

Build your learning

Students should research a major international event such as the Olympic Games and assess the importance of the event. Get them to research numbers of participants, sponsorship, promotion, numbers of visitors and special holiday deals. Students should also note any facilities that have been constructed especially for the event and assess how the construction – or the event itself –benefits the host country. Possible disadvantages of hosting international events should also be considered.

Session 6

Textbook pages 181 to 183

Resources required

- Holiday brochures and guide books
- Travel timetables
- Access to the internet

Objectives of session

- To explain the characteristics of tourist destinations:
  (f) accommodation types
  (g) transport
  (h) access.

Development of textbook

- Students should be made aware of the variety of different forms of accommodation that may be used, such as youth hostels, camping sites, motels, hotels, guest houses, etc.

- Students should also be introduced to the differences between room only, bed and breakfast, half-board, full-board and all-inclusive. The advantages and disadvantages of each can be covered through scenarios. For example, a family on a full-board package might discover several restaurants that they want to try outside of the hotel complex, but may feel restricted as they have pre-purchased their meals as part of the holiday.
- The activity on page 182 looks at the issue of quality ratings and accommodation classification systems. Students may wish to compare the UK system against the French system in Figure 3.12. Students could be asked if they would support a European standard of accommodation and what problems and benefits it would bring.
- The type and cost of transport to the holiday destination is briefly introduced in this session. A brainstorm is a good way to identify the main forms of transport. Comments on cost, levels of luxury and suitability could be made or drawn up as a table.
- Choose a holiday destination, such as Paris, and ask students to find out how many forms of transport can be used to get there. Details on company name, time taken to travel, cost, departure and arrival points should also be noted. It may also be useful to show students how to find out about travel times and routes apart from using brochures. For example, how would they find out if a flight had been delayed or cancelled?
- Students might also consider the level of services and facilities available on different forms of transport. The list describing facilities on ferries (see page 182) could be compared to a long-haul flight.

Key words to define

Accommodation, type and costs of transport, access.

Answers to textbook activities

Page 182: It is best if you select a variety of brochures beforehand so that not all students are looking at the same system of representing quality. If setting this as a piece of research, students should be told to collect brochures from at least three different tour operators. Note that within one brochure there may be different ways of representing quality, such as a star rating system, customer feedback, quotations, price, local accommodation ratings and written description in the brochure. Students can compare how different companies assess quality of hotels and resorts. Are they comparable? Suggest how a travel agent can use this information.

Build your learning

Students should read back through pages 174 to 183 before attempting the 'build your learning' activity on page 183. The destinations are best researched beforehand. A good selection of travel guides with supporting information from holiday brochures should be sufficient. In terms of statistics, students may refer to pages 160 to 161 and also to the websites listed in the resource and internet directory on page 463. Some of these statistical sites appear complex and therefore should be viewed before attempting to use them with students.

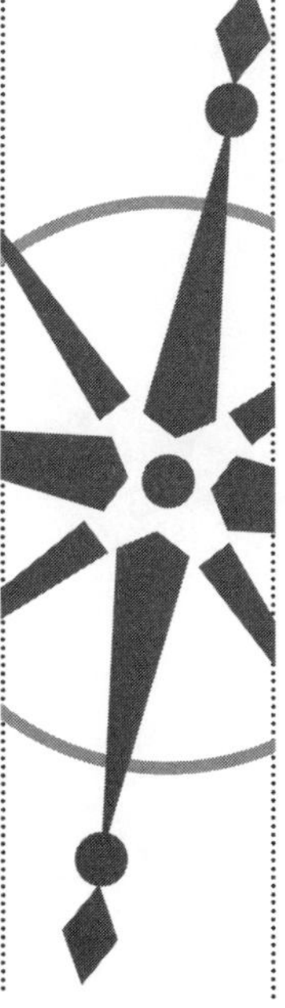

Session 7

Textbook pages 184 to 186

Resources required

- Atlas
- Travel guides

Objectives of session

To identify the main travel and tourism gateways.

Development of textbook

- Students should be able to understand what a gateway is, identify the main types of gateways and assess their relative importance. This could link in to a discussion on transport infrastructures leading to an agreed definition of terms such as airports, seaports, etc. Students may also wish to investigate the range of facilities required at a terminal and compare facilities for the different types of gateway – seaport, airport, railway station, border crossing.
- A way to explore the importance of gateways is to choose a country and ask students, using an atlas, to suggest how many ways a person may enter the country. They can then be asked to consider how difficult it would be to enforce or police the country's borders. This could then lead on to a discussion of border controls and the Schengen Treaty. Students may wish to find out why passports are needed, to review the relationship between the UK and Europe, and to understand when and where it is required to show a British passport.
- Outline the use of three letter codes for airports, and the use of secondary codes if there is more than one airport serving the same city. Suggest why the codes are in use as an introduction to the activity on page 185. The airports identified in Figure 3.14 could be located and mapped.

Key words to define

Travel routes, gateway, transport infrastructure, terminal, Schengen Treaty.

Answers to textbook activities

Page 185 'The world's busiest airports': Students should use an atlas or travel guide to locate the major centres of population that each airport serves. One of the reasons why the top ten airports receive so many passengers is that they are at the centre of huge transport hubs which connect air, road, rail and, sometimes, sea networks. The USA has most of the world's busiest airports because of the vast numbers of internal passenger arrivals and because the airports also serve large urban centres of population.

Page 185 'European airports': Most major airports use airport codes which are based on the city name, for example DUB is Dublin. However, where there is more than one airport secondary names are used: so LHR is London Heathrow. The airport codes shown on the map are listed here.

- United Kingdom – LHR, London Heathrow; LGW, London Gatwick; STN, Stansted; LCY, London City Airport; LTN, Luton; BHX, Birmingham; CWL, Cardiff; MAN, Manchester; NCL, Newcastle; EDI, Edinburgh; ABZ, Aberdeen; GLA, Glasgow; BFS, Belfast.
- Republic of Ireland – DUB, Dublin; ORK, Cork; SNN, Shannon; NOC, Knock.
- France – LIL, Lille; LEH, Le Havre; CDG, Charles de Gaulle; ORY, Orly; RNS, Reims; NTE, Nantes; BOD, Bordeaux; LDE, Lourdes; CFE, Clermont-Ferrand; TLS, Toulouse; MRS, Marseille; NCE, Nice; LYS, Lyon; AJA, Ajaccio.
- Spain – MAD, Madrid; BIO, Bilbao; SCQ, Santiago de Compostela; BCN, Barcelona; VLC, Valencia; ALC, Alicante; AGP, Málaga; SVQ, Seville; IBZ, Ibiza; PMI, Palma de Mallorca; MAH, Mahón; GIB, Gibraltar (UK).
- Portugal – OPO, Oporto; LIS, Lisbon; FAO, Faro.
- Italy – TRN, Turin; MXP, Malpensa (Milan); LIN, Linate (Milan); GOA, Genoa; PSA, Pisa; FCO, Rome; NAP, Naples; BLQ, Bologna; VCE, Venice; PMO, Palermo; CTA, Catánia; CAG, Cágliari.
- Malta – MLA, Malta.
- Greece – CFU, Corfu.
- Switzerland – GVA, Geneva; BRN, Berne; BSL, Basle; ZRH, Zurich.
- Austria – INN, Innsbruck; SZG, Salzburg; LNZ, Linz; VIE, Vienna; KLU, Klagenfurt.
- Germany – MUC, Munich; AGB, Augsburg; NUE, Nuremburg; STR, Stuttgart; FRA, Frankfurt; SCN, Saabrücken; CGN, Cologne; DUS, Düsseldorf; FMO, Münster; DRS, Dresden; LEJ, Leipzig; HAJ, Hannover; SXF, Berlin Schönefeld; TXL, Berlin Tegel; HAM, Hamburg; BRE, Bremen.
- Luxembourg – LUX, Luxembourg.
- Netherlands – GRQ, Groningen; ENS, Enschede; EIN, Eindhoven; AMS, Amsterdam; RTM, Rotterdam.
- Belgium – ANR, Antwerp; BRU, Brussels; LGG, Liège; OST, Ostend.

SESSION PLANS

- Denmark – AAR, Aarhus.
- Sweden – MMX, Malmö; JKG, Jönköping; GOT, Gothenburg; ARN, Stockholm; SDL, Sundsvall.
- Norway – TRD, Trondheim; FBU, Oslo; KRS, Kristiansand; SVG, Stavanger; BGO, Bergen.

Build your learning

Using a travel atlas or list of airports, get students to identify the main airports not located on the map on page 185, focusing on Greece and Turkey in particular. Students may wish to add some of the main air routes from one main UK airport to ten short-haul and ten long-haul destinations. Flight information can be found using brochures, flight timetables, Teletext and the internet, see for example www.baa.co.uk.

Session 8

Textbook pages 186 to 191

Resources required

- European road atlas
- Access to the internet
- Holiday brochures

Objectives of session

To identify the main travel routes that tourists use when travelling to their holiday destinations.

Development of textbook

- Students should be introduced to the main travel routes, both short haul and long haul. This is best achieved by the use of maps and timetable information.
- The advantages and disadvantages of each type of transport should be explored, along with an assessment of varying levels of service, speed and comfort. Students should be asked for their preferred method of travel to a host of given destinations. Types of transport are outlined on page 186.
- Students may not have heard about the European International Network (E numbers) used on European road networks. This should be explained with a discussion as to why the UK has not adopted the system. Answers to the activity on page 187 should be given in terms of both A and E road numbers.
- Students often regard the flight to a holiday destination as the sole mode of transport and do not often think about the transfers at either end. Transfers should be explored, not just those by chartered bus but also transfers by taxi, scheduled bus, rail and air services.
- Using the newspaper extract on page 190, explore cross-Channel competition. Students can research the various ways in which companies are trying to attract customers. The impact of the Channel Tunnel upon European travel is important, although students should be reminded that it is not just ferry companies and train operators that are competing for business, but also airlines and sea catamarans.

Key words to define

European International Network, scheduled flights, special group inclusive tours (SGITS), inclusive tours by excursion (ITX), charter flights, inclusive tours by charter (ITC), sea catamaran.

Answers to textbook activities

Page 187:

- Calais to Paris – A26/E15 to Arras, A1/E15 to Paris
- Calais to Brussels – A16/E40 to Dunkerque, A25/E42 to Lille, A8 to Halle, A7 to Brussels; or A16/E40 to Oostende, A10/E40 to Brussels
- Calais to Salzburg – A26/E15 Calais to Arras, A26/E17 Arras to Reims, A4/E50 Reims to Metz, A4/E25 Metz to Karlsruhe, A8/E52 Karlsruhe to Stuttgart, A8/E52 Stuttgart to Munich, A8/E52 Munich to Salzburg

Several route planners exist on the internet including www.reiseroute.de/europ_uk.htm, www.michelin-travel.com and www.rac.co.uk.

Page 188: This activity is best done by using holiday brochures. Although students may use an atlas, they should go through the process of searching for published information from tour operators and travel principals. Combinations of travel types should also be identified.

Build your learning

The build your learning activity on page 191 is best researched from holiday brochures, atlases and travel guides. The question hints at there being more than one route or form of transport to a particular holiday destination. Students should be encouraged to note all options. Routes can be chosen from convenient departure points local to the students. Gateways may vary depending on the departure points and form of transport used. The final task requires a comparison to be made of several routes. The information will probably be best researched from holiday brochures and from the internet. There may be a relationship between the answers given: for example, the quickest or the most comfortable route may also be the most expensive.

Session 9

Textbook pages 192 to 193

Resources required

- Copy of exchange rates from a recent newspaper
- Advertisements for budget airlines

Objectives of session

- To explain the fluctuating popularity of tourist destinations caused by:
  (a) economic factors.

Development of textbook

- This session begins a study of why different resorts become popular while others become less popular. It links in with the product life cycle concept (see page 246). Fluctuating popularity can be explained in terms of economic, social and political, environmental and geographical factors. This session focuses on economic reasons.
- The cost of holidays should be defined, and may be displayed showing the different types of costs involved. The rise in budget airlines should be explained, and students might analyse the affect this phenomenon has had on the travel market. Has this lead to a decrease in holiday costs, if so why?
- Exchange rates require careful explanation. The summary on pages 192 and 193 introduces the ideas, and it is worthwhile going through this step by step. A detailed explanation is not required here, however you should emphasise the effects of rising costs and changes in the value of the pound.
- The term inflation also needs defining and you might review the impact of inflation on the tourist industry. You should make the point that inflation occurs in other countries not just our own.

Key words to define

Cost of holiday, exchange rate, rate of inflation.

Answers to textbook activities

Page 192: Budget airlines include Go and easyJet, and airfares may be found in brochures, on websites or through newspaper advertisements. Impacts on tourist destinations should include an assessment of perceived accessibility, numbers of visitors, types of visitors, length of stay, increased revenue, competition with traditional carriers, investment in infrastructure and services.

Page 193 'Impact of exchange rates on travel': Question 1 – the Euro is not a national currency. Question 2 – people travelling throughout Europe will be able to use the same currency, will not have to carry a lot of different currency in their pockets, will be able to compare prices easier, and can avoid conversion between currencies and currency commission rates. Question 3 – exchange rates are found in most

newspapers. Make sure students read page 193 before answering the question. The countries in which the pound is strong, and therefore buys more local currency, will benefit UK tourists as goods appear cheaper.

Page 193 'Price of holidays': Question 1 – the most expensive destination is Barbados. Students should give examples and comment on other items which appear expensive. Question 2 – everyone wants value for money but Barbados buys exclusivity. Try to avoid the use of stereotypes. Question 3 – prices vary due to the costs of living and production, local wages, competition, exchange rates and items priced to meet the expectations of visiting tourists. Question 4 – some countries appear to be exclusive and therefore attract attention. Resorts which are value for money attracts lots of tourists, but the cheapest resorts do not necessarily attract people who are going to spend large amounts of money. If a resort is seen to be too expensive, tourists will tend to look for alternative destinations.

Build your learning

Using a CD-ROM broadsheet newspaper archive, students should research news items that combine stories based on economy and tourism. General issues should be noted as well as examples. They should produce a detailed study on one particular country.

Session 10

Textbook pages 194 to 199

Resources required

- Holiday brochures from student travel companies
- Access to the internet

Objectives of session

- To explain the fluctuating popularity of tourist destinations caused by:
  (b) social and political factors.

Development of textbook

- It is important that students have good examples of how political and social events affect the popularity of tourist destinations. Start by introducing and defining the main social and political factors. Students can then use the textbook to provide suitable examples. Groups of students could be given a factor to research and report back to the rest of the class. There are many activities within this session that can be given to different groups of students.
- Students should focus on current examples. By looking at media coverage, they can research current events and expand their knowledge on tourist destinations that are in the news. Destinations may be newsworthy for several reasons and this, in itself, can serve to draw together the various strands that impact on the popularity of a tourist destination.
- Tourism management is an important factor in its own right. The criteria on page 197 of the textbook can be applied to local examples or to tourist destinations that are familiar to students. Does the case study on page 198 fit all of the criteria?
- Introduce the activity on page 199 as a build your learning activity. This forms the basis of the assessment for this unit and therefore serves as an exercise in planning ahead and building up a range of information about students' chosen destinations.

Key words to define

Promoting holiday destinations, exclusivity, over-commercialisation, level of crime, political instability, media coverage, tourism management, independent travel.

Answers to textbook activities

Page 194: Students might select a tourist destination such as Ibiza or Benidorm. Explanations could include rapid and mass development of high-rise hotels and commercial outlets with little regard for local

culture or history. The effects have been to transform existing settlements into large-scale tourist resorts. Many Spanish resorts were humble fishing villages fifty years ago and have since grown into 'Europe's playground'. Ibiza and other similar resorts have developed a reputation for fun and escapism, alcohol and sex. The reality for tourism managers is that the people these resorts attract do not spend vast amounts of money, and therefore resorts on the Costa Del Sol – and other similar resorts – are now trying to attract a different type of tourist who is prepared to spend more money. The 'lager lout' image can not be sustained. Even Ibiza is now selling itself as a quality party and music venue, not one of cheap alcohol.

Page 196 'Luxor': The massacre frightened many people into thinking that Luxor, and Egypt, was unsafe for British tourists. The reputation of Egypt was reduced as people saw that they could be hurt by a terrorist campaign and many people cancelled their holidays or chose alternative holiday destinations. Much press coverage ensured that Egypt developed negative image as newspapers perpetuated the story of a terrorist campaign against tourists. Since the incident, the Egyptian Government has increased the level of security and also restricted terrorist activities. During the last couple of years the price of holidays to Egypt has fallen and, with an advertising campaign by the national tourist office, more people are travelling back to Egypt as confidence is restored.

Page 196 'The Kosovo Crisis': Other areas were affected by the Kosovo crisis by the threat of trouble in neighbouring areas and by the ignorance of potential tourists, who did not know which areas were affected by the conflict. They may also fear that countries such as Italy might become further involved in the crisis and become targets for revenge attacks.

By promoting tourism and reassuring the public that there is no threat to tourists, people may be prepared to visit or at least not cancel their holidays. An approach of saying little and not offering reassurance is likely to see a drop in visitor numbers.

Warnings about travelling to the Balkans were issued by the Foreign and Commonwealth Office and travel agents gave out advice. Although some holidays to Italy and Turkey were cancelled, the tourist industry promoted these areas offering discounts on the price of a holiday.

Page 197: It is best for students to find out about a country of their choice or a predetermined set of countries. Trouble spots should be highlighted by the exercise. Comparisons can be made between information given by various governments. It is best to start with the Foreign and Commonwealth Office website www.fco.gov.uk/travel/

Page 198: The solar eclipse was a unique experience; some people observed it for the spectacle whilst others witnessed it for religious reasons. There was huge demand for special eclipse glasses, and a tourist demand to witness the event at special sites. Sites included those able to give the best view such as in Cornwall, and religious and sacred sites such as Avebury and Stonehenge. The eclipse generated a mass advertising and merchandising campaign and a large-scale exercise in tourism management.

With hot and sunny weather, there would have been more people attending the eclipse in Cornwall, and a greater amount of celebration and purchase of merchandise. Bednights in Cornwall would have increased, with greater road congestion as four million people were expected to arrive over a few days. Without effective tourism management, the worries highlighted in the article may have come true. If there had been a problem then, with the high media coverage, any stories of poor planning would have reported to the nation.

A final question could be added asking the students whether they thought the eclipse was a good example of tourism management, and if not, why?

Page 199: Access to brochures or the internet is a useful starting point. Main routes and gateways to two short-haul and two long-haul destinations will depend on the destinations chosen. Appeal to students would include value for money, friendly advice on hand, fun and lively destination.

Build your learning

The activity on page 199 requires students to select two short-haul and two long-haul destinations. This is to prepare students for the end of section activity on page 202, and you should allow students to begin gathering relevant information in order to plan ahead.

Session 11

Textbook pages 199 to 202

Resources required

- Access to the internet
- Travel brochures

Objectives of session

- To explain the fluctuating popularity of tourist destinations caused by:
  (c) geographical and environmental factors.
- To identify the main transport principals serving a destination.

Development of textbook

- This session focuses on the geographical factors influencing the popularity of tourist destinations. The main terms should be defined, with examples from short-haul and long-haul destinations. Although there is some overlap with material on natural attractions on pages 177 to 178, the focus here is on the changing popularity of destinations in terms of their location.
- Access to destinations can change, becoming easier with new routes and forms of transport, or less accessible through increased traffic disruption. Through student discussion, a table can be drawn up outlining the ways in which access to resorts may be enhanced or limited by various actions.
- Changing climatic conditions might be perceived by students as freak weather and provide examples of storms, floods and extreme snow fall. Few regard rising temperatures as a problem in tourist resorts.
- Pollution is a major problem that can affect all tourist destinations. Some examples of pollution and the ways that it affects various tourist destinations are outlined on page 200 of the textbook. Students may list different types of pollution and explain how they potentially affect tourist destinations. An assessment should be made as to whether these different types of pollution would have a major impact on the tourism levels.
- A straightforward way to measure the popularity of a destination, without the use of statistics, is to assess the numbers of transport principals serving a particular resort. The relative popularity of both short-haul and long-haul destinations may be compared in this way. Note that this approach does have some obvious problems: it may not necessarily explain the relative volume of traffic and that a holiday destination may have more than one gateway. Using a selection of destinations, students might list the main transport principals.

Key words to define

Access, climatic conditions, water quality, natural disasters, transport principals.

Answers to textbook activities

Page 201 'Unsafe beaches': Although this extract refers to several beaches, the article's main focus is on Dawlish Warren in Devon. The image created is one of pollution, harmful bacteria, general pollution and poor management. However, the article ignores the positive aspects of these resorts and fails to report on any good practice that is taking place. It is debatable who is responsible – polluters, public or beach managers? There may be little impact on tourists who frequent the beach but others may stay away and visit alternative locations. As a result, the article may harm tourist numbers for seasons to come.

Page 201 Turkish earthquake: The disaster affected the Turkish tourist industry as many people thought it was unsafe to visit the country. They feared the threat of another earthquake or aftershock. They

perceived mass damage to hotels and tourist infrastructure across Turkey and were worried that even in unaffected areas local people would be in a state of shock or would be too preoccupied to worry about tourists. In reality, the tourist destinations to the south of Turkey were untouched by the earthquake but bookings took a dramatic slump with cheap deals being introduced the following year to try and restore consumer confidence.

To find out about the risk of earthquakes and problem areas in general contact the Foreign and Commonwealth Office or consult websites that deal specifically with earthquakes, such as www.geo.ed.ac/quakes/quakes.html and www.gsrg.nmh.ac.uk. Note that, in the first instance, a travel agent should pass on details about places that pose a danger before a booking is made.

Build your learning

The end of section activity is based around the two short-haul and two long-haul destinations chosen by students for the overall assessment for this unit. Students should explain recent developments which have taken place under the headings suggested. It is important that students support their findings with statistics and factual material. The main travel principals can be identified from brochures and from research on the internet (see the internet and resource directory on pages 460 to 464).

Sessions 12 and 13

Textbook pages 203 to 210

Resources required

- OHTs 1, 2 and 3
- Brochures
- Access to the internet
- Travel guides and a travel atlas
- Geographical digest

Objectives of session

- To produce assessment evidence for the unit.
- To investigate and examine two short-haul destinations, examples include Spain and France.

Development of textbook

- The end of unit assessment should be discussed in depth (see pages 454 to 455). Students should be able to explain what each part of the assessment requires and know where they are going to locate the information to complete the set tasks. Two sessions have been allocated for this process, one for each of the two case studies.
- Use OHT 1 to discuss methods of best practice when researching information. Ensure that sources are relevant and are as recent as possible. Students should make themselves familiar with these information sources as they underpin the requirements of the assessment.
- Students should discuss the best methods of presenting information. Read through pages 203 to 206 and discuss different ways that information can be presented. Students should consider, for example, using annotated maps, graphs, photographs and visual images.
- Discuss the format of the report. Come to an agreement with students about whether they should produce the assessment in a traditional report format or apply the assessment criteria to produce a detailed travel guide or other form of presentation. It is important for both students and tutors to be aware that the assessment is focused on identification, explanation, analysis and interpretation; many students may tend to rely upon description which is only a small part of the assessment.
- Students should be made aware that examples and statistics are best used to support their comments. However it is important that the assessment criteria is adhered to at all times. Students should be aware of the difference between the requirements for grades E, C and A.

SESSION PLANS

- To complete the first task of the assessment, students are required to identify and describe, using a map, the location of the chosen destinations. The maps on pages 203 and 207 are for illustration only; OHTs 2 and 3 providing maps of Spain and Paris are more detailed. Students should be able to locate features using an atlas. In addition, they may wish to mark on their maps physical features, such as lakes, mountain ranges, and any built attractions like theme parks and castles.
- Students can use the travel files presented in the textbook as a basis for their assessments, but recommend that they use additional sources of information. Students may also decide to research two short-haul destinations of their own choice.

Answers to textbook activities and indexes to maps

Page 206: The activity is best carried out after an initial search through a variety of brochures. The last question asks students to provide costings based on the brochure. Although this has not been a focus of the unit, it provides the opportunity to apply information on travel routes and gateways as well as generate evidence for key skills in application of number.

Page 209: As the number and range of events in Paris is so enormous, the activity asks students to research the latest information using the internet so that they find up-to-date examples.

Page 210: The activity is based around a planned group visit to Paris. This has been chosen as many schools and colleges use Paris as a base for foreign residential visits and such a visit could form the basis of this activity. The activity covers travel routes and gateways, asking students to justify why these were chosen. An itinerary is required: students must decide what appeal the city has to UK tourists and to select potential attractions, events, entertainment and accommodation.

Sydney and Melbourne map (OHT 2): Snowy Mountains (1), Bowral (2), Mittagong (3), Katoomba (4), Ku-Ring-Gai Chase National Park (5), Gosford/Terrigal (6), Hunter Valley (7), Blue Mountains (8), Newcastle (9), Central Coast (10), Wollongong (11), Botany Bay (12), Kiama (13) and Kingsford Smith Airport (14).

Barbados map (OHT 3): Garrison (1), Hastings (2), Oistins Bay (3), Grantley Adams Airport (4), Flower Forest (5), Chalky Hill (6), Barbados Wildlife Reserve (7), Folkstone Underwater Park (8), Mt Hillaby (9) and Harrisons Cave (10).

Build your learning

Students should refine their research techniques and agree on a format in order to complete the end of unit assessment. Some statistics are given in the tables on pages 160 and 161; other data can be obtained from national tourist offices and from websites (see the end of each travel file section). Students might also use a newspaper CD-ROM archive from a library to search for recent articles and statistics on tourism in their chosen countries. A geographical digest also gives statistical information by country.

Sessions 14 and 15

Textbook pages 211 to 215

Resources required

- OHTs 4, 5 and 6
- Brochures
- Access to the internet
- Travel guides and travel atlas

Objectives of session

- To produce assessment evidence for the unit.
- To investigate and examine two long-haul destinations, choosing two from North America, the Caribbean and Australasia.

Development of textbook

- The textbook provides three travel files, though only two destinations are required for assessment purposes. Students may wish to research other long-haul destinations of their own choice. The report format should follow the style agreed in the last two sessions. Again two sessions have been allocated, one for each of the two case studies.
- In order to complete the first task of the assessment, students are required to identify and describe, using a map, the location of the chosen destinations. As the maps on pages 211, 217 and 221 are for illustration only, use the more detailed maps of North America, Barbados and Australia on OHTs 4, 5 and 6, respectively. Students should be able to locate features using an atlas. In addition, they may wish to mark on their maps physical features, such as lakes, mountain ranges, and any built attractions like theme parks and castles.

Answers to textbook activities and indexes to maps

Page 215: Most brochures provide a good indication of why Florida is popular with UK tourists. However, students sometimes need to be reminded that their own reports require a critical approach rather than simply rewriting a marketing document. The itinerary helps to focus the student and covers the main points of the assessment, and it presents opportunities for key skills in application of number. A discussion of the factors that have resulted in Florida becoming a popular holiday resort should be supported using examples and statistics.

Page 220: The activity asks for an itinerary to be drawn up, requiring a detailed knowledge of the island, gateways and major transport principals. The second part asks the student to discuss in report format how the island has developed as a centre for tourism. The question goes beyond a description of these changes, but asks that the student to draw conclusions about the future of tourism on the island. Students should be encouraged to use Figure 3.24 on page 216.

Page 225: The activity uses the tourist arrival data in Figure 3.28 on page 221. The rate of change is best described numerically using a range of examples and methods of presentation. The last part of the activity requires an itinerary for a student about to embark on a working holiday in Australia. There is information provided by USIT and the Student Travel Association about working abroad and the most cost-effective methods of travel and accommodation. Visa requirements and latest travel information can be obtained from the Foreign and Commonwealth Office website (see page 197).

Florida map (OHT 4): Key West (1), Everglades National Park (2), Big Cyprus National Reserve (3), Clearwater (4), Daytona Beach (5), John F Kennedy Space Centre (6), Cape Canaveral (7), Universal Studios Florida (8), Sea World of Florida (9), Kissimmee (10), Walt Disney World (11), Lake Okeechobee (12), Belle Glade (13), Palm Beach (14), Fort Lauderdale (15), Hollywood (16) and Miami Beach (17).

Costa Blanca map (OHT 5): Campello (1), Villajoyosa (2), Finestrat (3), Alfaz de Pi (4), Calpe (5), Guadaleste (6), Moraira (7), Teulada (8), Penon de Ifach (9) and Mediterranean Sea (10).

Paris map (OHT 6): Chartres (1), Versailles (2), St-Denis (3), Beauvais (4), Compeigne (5), Parc Asterix (6), Charles de Gaulle (7), Le Bourget (8), Disneyland Paris (9), Orly (10), Nanterre (11) and Champigny-sur-Marne (12).

Build your learning

Students should continue to refine their research techniques in completing the end of unit assessment. Long-haul destinations gives the opportunity for students to research holiday resorts that may be unfamiliar to them, and this may therefore require a little more time in the collection and interpretation of information. Before handing in the completed report make sure that it covers all the required assessment criteria and meets the expectations of the assessor.

Research skills

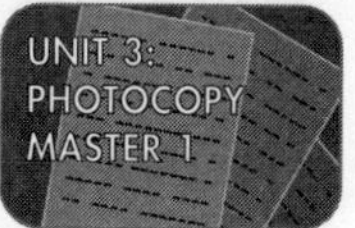

Everyone in the travel and tourism industry needs to be able to use research skills to obtain information for their work or to provide accurate and up-to-date information to customers.

Research involves:

- being clear about what you are trying to find out
- knowing how to search for information
- deciding what might be useful
- collecting and presenting relevant information
- drawing conclusions about your findings
- acknowledging your sources

You need to use your research skills to build up your knowledge and understanding of travel destinations. Those already working in the travel and tourism industry expect you to know how to carry out research using a variety of sources including:

- primary sources (for example, people, working in travel and tourism, customers)
- secondary sources (for example, gazetteers, brochures, maps, atlases, guidebooks, textbooks, the internet, newspapers and trade journals)

It is important that you become familiar with using a variety of sources of information.

UNIT 3: PHOTOCOPY MASTER 2

Costa Blanca, Spain

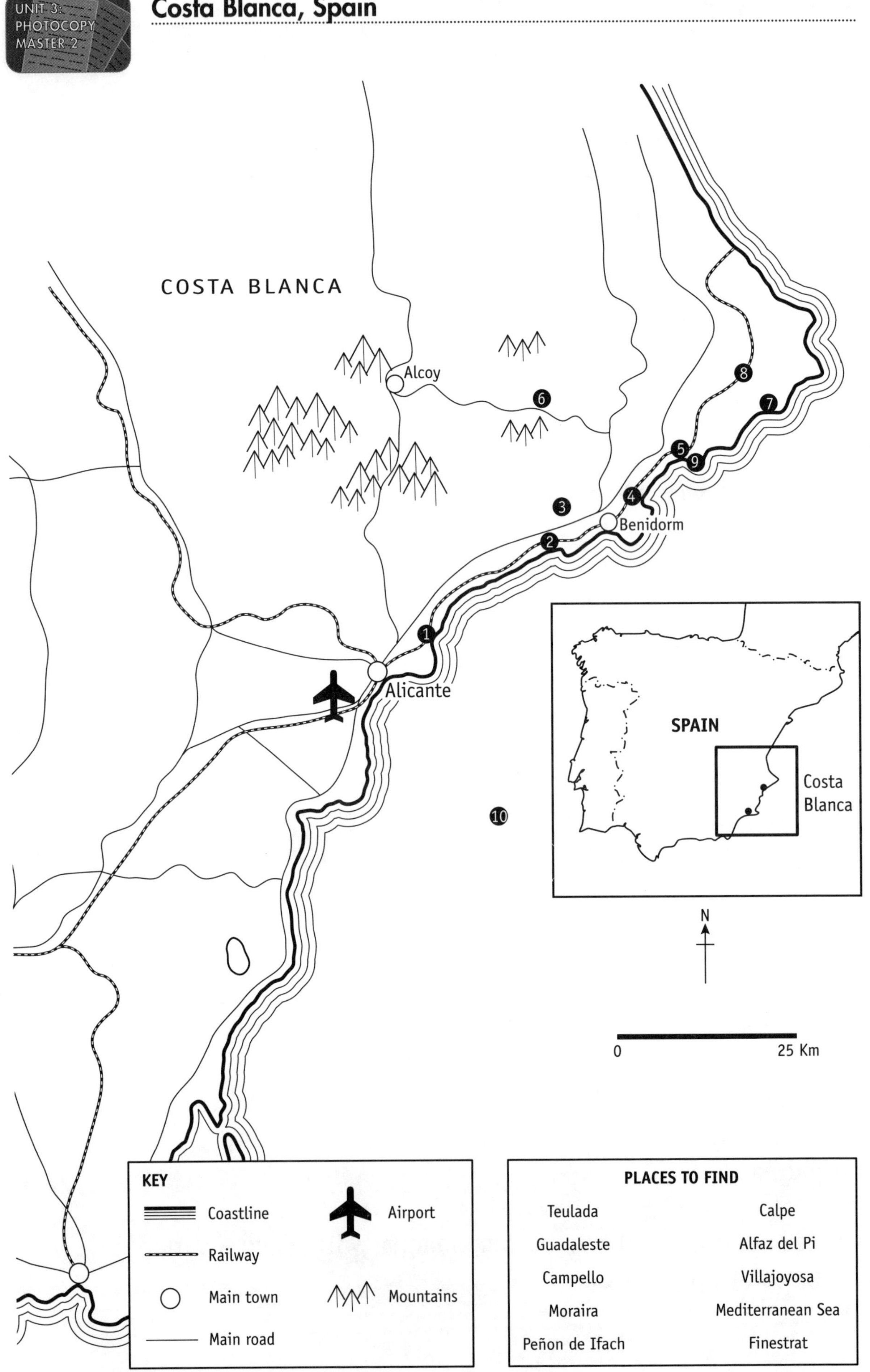

PLACES TO FIND

Teulada	Calpe
Guadaleste	Alfaz del Pi
Campello	Villajoyosa
Moraira	Mediterranean Sea
Peñon de Ifach	Finestrat

Paris

UNIT 3: PHOTOCOPY MASTER 3

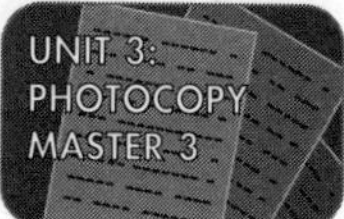

Paris
France
N
R. Seine
1
2
3
4
5
6
7
8
9
10
11
12
13
PARIS
R. Seine
0
30 Km

KEY

River Seine	Airport
Railway	Built up area
Capital city	Town
Main road	

PLACES TO FIND

Beauvais	Compiègne
Chartres	St-Denis
Versailles	Nanterre
Disneyland Paris	Champigny-sur-Marne
Parc Astérix	Orly
Charles de Gaulle	Fontainebleau
Le Bourget	

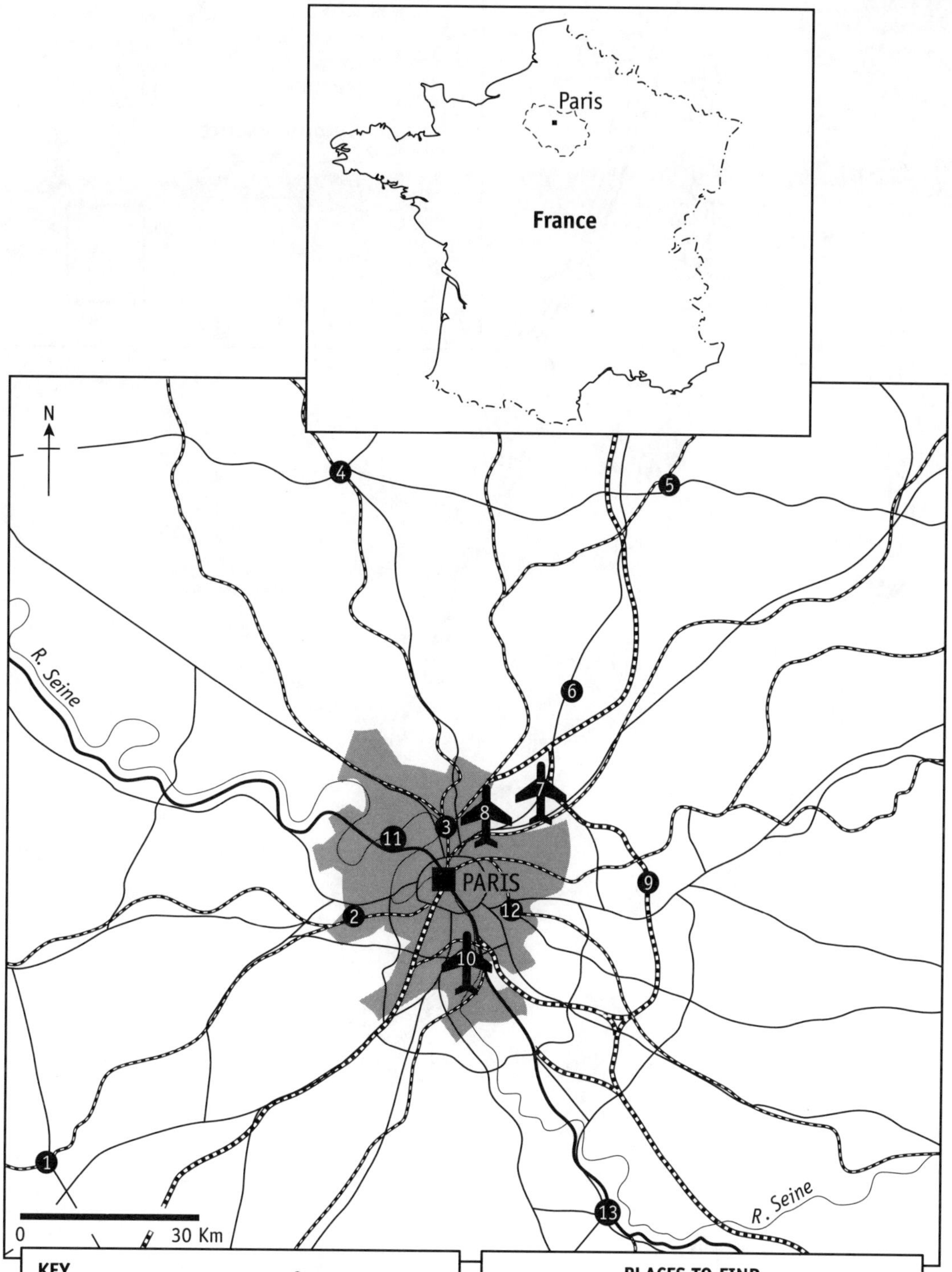

UNIT 3: PHOTOCOPY MASTER 4

Florida

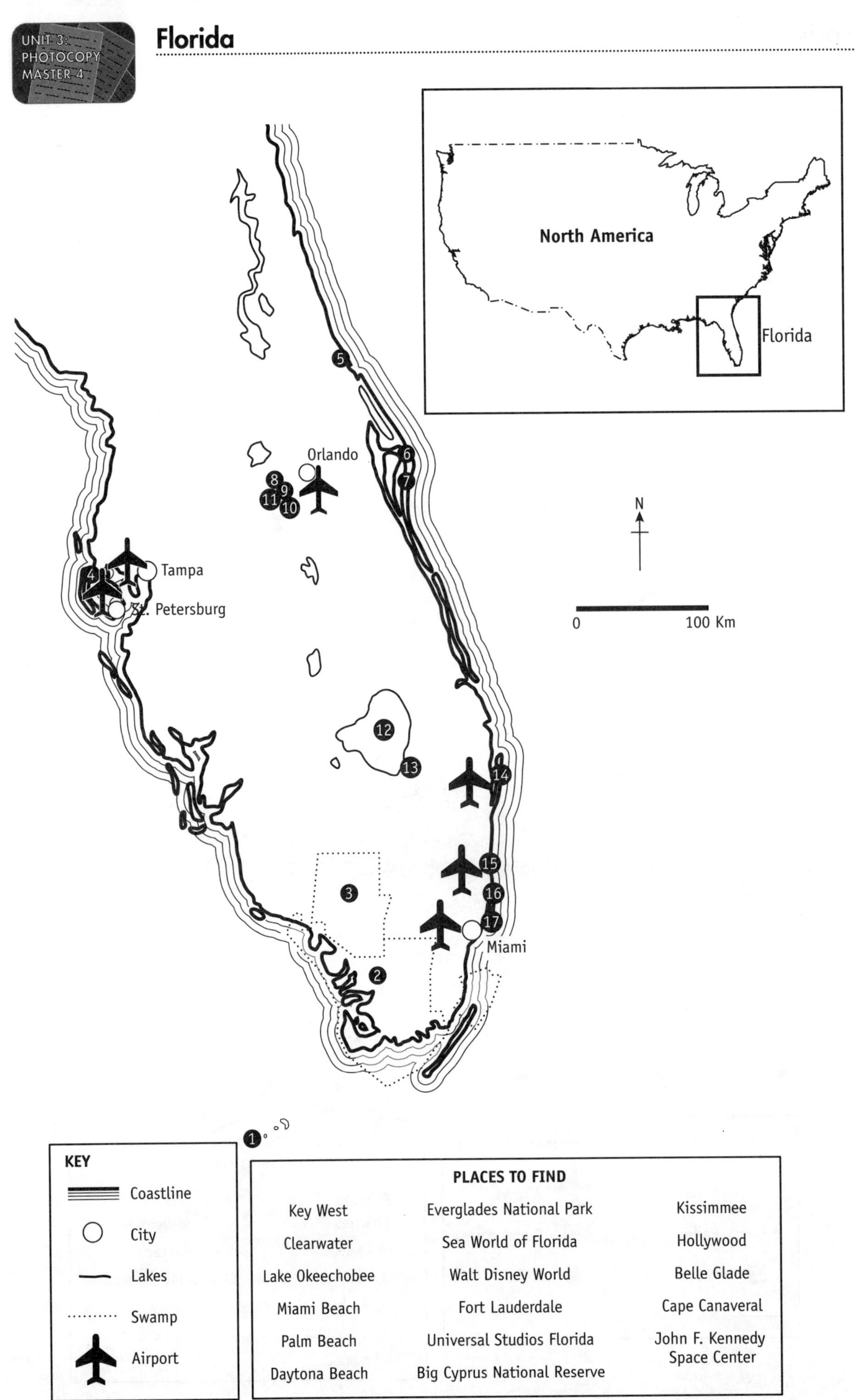

Barbados

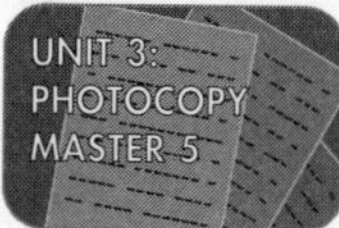

UNIT 3: PHOTOCOPY MASTER 5

Barbados
Speightsdown
BRIDGETOWN
1
2
3
4
5
6
7
8
9
10
N
0
5 Km

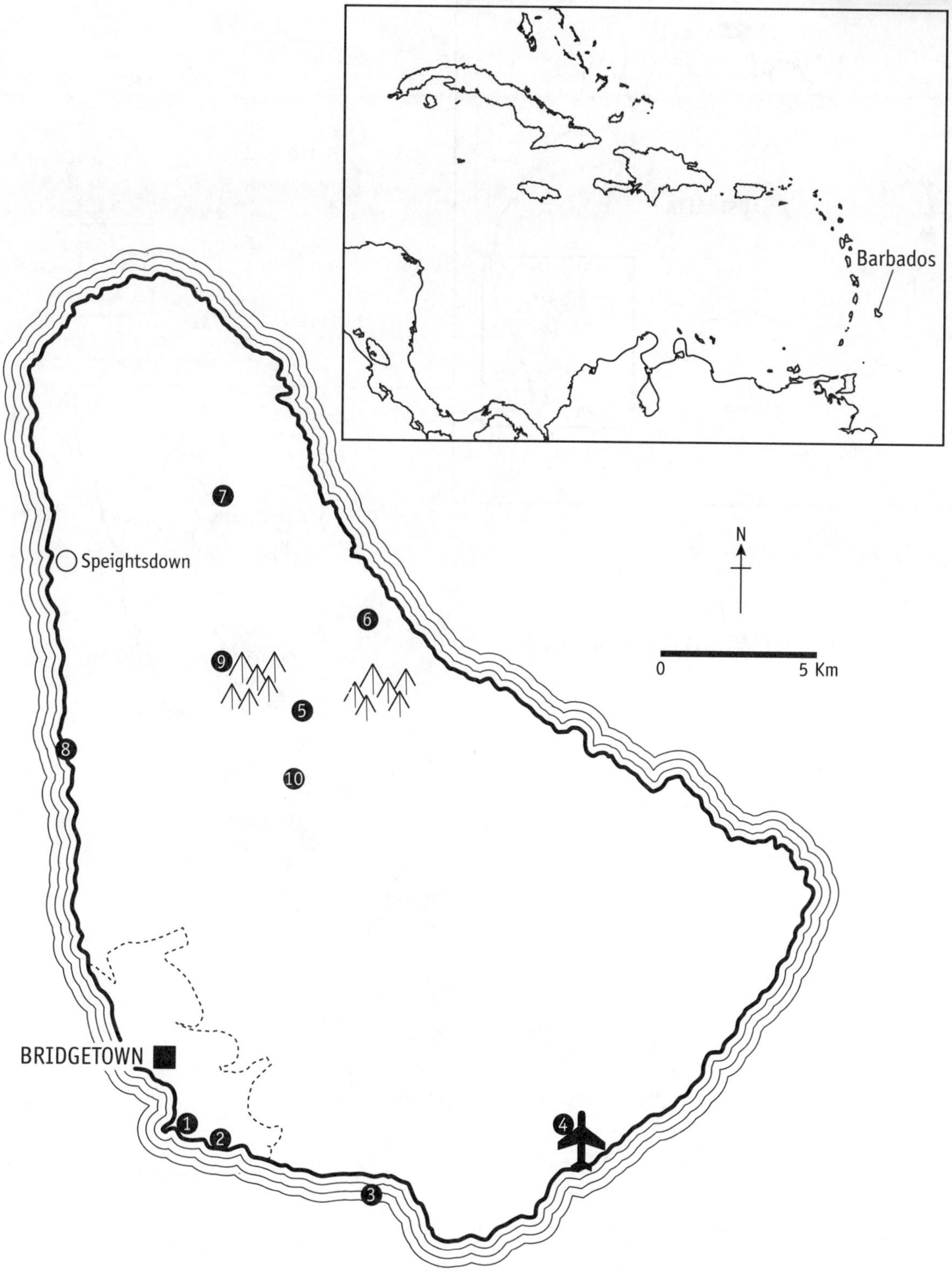

KEY

- Coastline
- Capital
- Mountains
- Airport

PLACES TO FIND

Grantley Adams	Folkstone Underwater Park
Garrison	Mt Hillaby
Oistins Bay	Flower Forest
Chalkly Hill	Hastings
Barbados Wildlife Reserve	Harrison's Cave

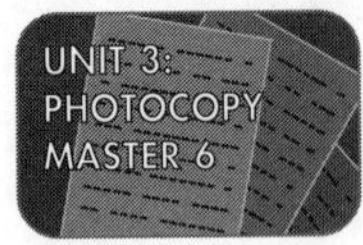

Sydney and Melbourne

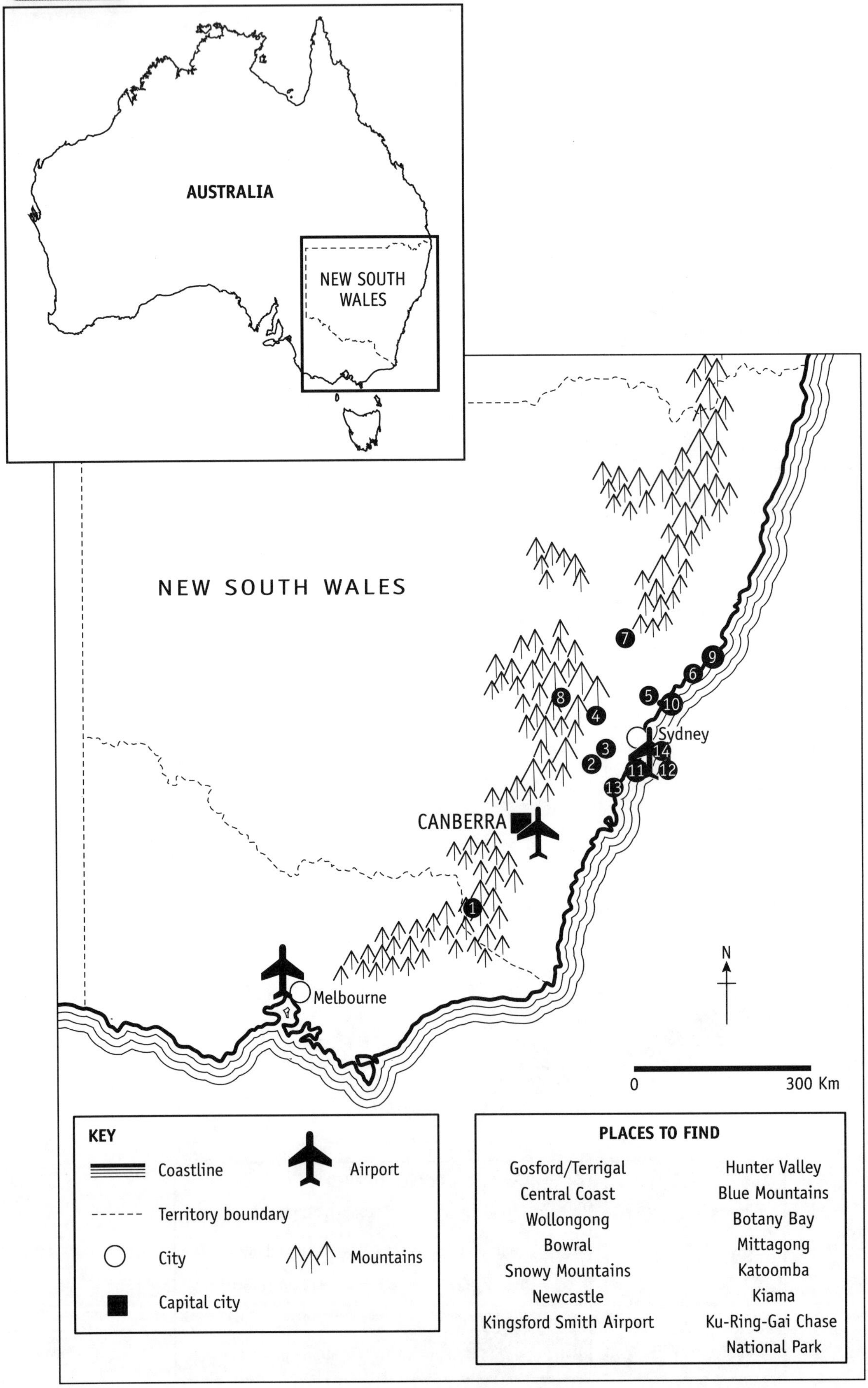

AUSTRALIA

NEW SOUTH WALES

NEW SOUTH WALES

CANBERRA

Sydney

Melbourne

1 2 3 4 5 6 7 8 9 10 11 12 13 14

N

0 300 Km

KEY

- Coastline
- Territory boundary
- City
- Capital city
- Airport
- Mountains

PLACES TO FIND

Gosford/Terrigal	Hunter Valley
Central Coast	Blue Mountains
Wollongong	Botany Bay
Bowral	Mittagong
Snowy Mountains	Katoomba
Newcastle	Kiama
Kingsford Smith Airport	Ku-Ring-Gai Chase National Park

Unit 4: Marketing in travel and tourism

Introduction

This unit introduces the use of marketing within the travel and tourism industries. For students that have completed the Intermediate GNVQ qualification in leisure and tourism, it will build on their knowledge and understanding of the marketing mix and the use of promotional materials and techniques.

Delivery suggestions

This unit contains a lot of marketing information and many terms that are likely to be new to most students. You might, therefore, suggest that students keep a glossary of marketing terms. Organised group visits and guest speakers are a useful way of allowing students to evaluate how marketing is used within the leisure and recreation industry. Students should be encouraged to identify, discuss and evaluate real examples of marketing activities within the industry and many of the activities within the textbook are designed for this purpose. This is particularly important as part of the preparation for the external assessment.

Links to other units

Unit 1

Marketing has strong links to investigating travel and tourism in terms of demonstrating the ways in which the individual components of the industry develop products and services to target different types of customers. Unit 1 also discusses the difference between products, services, events, facilities, etc, which can be linked to discussions on the 'product' element of the marketing mix.

Unit 2

Many of the textbook's case studies look at the marketing of travel and tourism products and services that have been recently developed. Students might explore the link between effective marketing and successful tourism development.

Unit 5

Students should understand that the 'product' element of the marketing mix often largely comprises excellent customer service. Students should also understand that the targeting of different market segments may influence the type of customer service offered.

Unit 6

Students can incorporate a marketing element into the internal assessment activity for this unit.

Unit planner

Session	Session objectives	Text pages
1	To introduce the topic of marketing, highlighting its importance for all travel and tourism providers To explain the importance of setting SMART marketing objectives	227 to 231
2	To explore the ways in which organisations analyse the internal (SWOT) and external (PEST) influences on the business environment	232 to 239
3	To identify and analyse the needs and expectations of customers in terms of targeting and positioning travel and tourism products and services To identify and discuss the product element of the marketing mix	239 to 246
4	To explain and discuss the ways in which the product life cycle influences the development of travel and tourism products and services To evaluate how the location or chain of distribution of travel and tourism products and services forms part of the marketing mix	246 to 251
5	To explain and discuss how travel and tourism organisations determine price and use pricing policies as part of their marketing mix	251 to 255
6	To introduce and discuss the general ways in which travel and tourism organisations use promotion as part of their marketing mix To identify how travel and tourism organisations can evaluate the effectiveness of their marketing mix	256 to 259
7	To define market research and its objectives To identify and explain how travel and tourism organisations classify customers into key segments	260 to 266
8	To explain and discuss how travel and tourism organisations conduct primary research	266 to 272
9	To explain and discuss how travel and tourism organisations conduct secondary research To discuss how research findings are analysed and how suitable research techniques are selected	273 to 281
10	To introduce and discuss how marketing communications are used by travel and tourism organisations To discuss the function of advertising within marketing communications	283 to 290
11	To explore how travel and tourism organisations use brochures and direct marketing as an effective part of their marketing communications	290 to 294
12	To explore how travel and tourism organisations use public relations and sales promotions as an effective part of marketing communications	294 to 302
13	To explore how travel and tourism organisations use sponsorship as an effective part of their marketing communications To discuss the ways in which AIDA and timing can affect the overall success of promotions	302 to 306
14	To explain and discuss the legal requirements involved in planning and using effective marketing communications	306 to 311
15	To prepare for the external unit assessment	

Session 1

Textbook pages 227 to 231

Resources required

- Handout of the Institute of Marketing's definition of marketing (on page 228 of the textbook)
- OHT 1

Objectives of session

- To introduce the topic of marketing, highlighting its importance for all travel and tourism providers.
- To explain the importance of setting SMART marketing objectives.

Development of textbook

- Brainstorming is a good way of introducing the topic of marketing. Students can be shown the Institute of Marketing's definition and then be asked to suggest the range of activities that marketing will include based on this definition. You can consolidate the students' ideas by using OHT 1 and discussing which activities fit into each of the six stages of the marketing process.
- Students need to understand the importance of setting objectives. You may ask them to consider why an organisation sets objectives. For example, they should identify that it allows an organisation to measure its performance against the set objectives. You may use the examples of objectives on page 231 of the text to illustrate how objectives need to be SMART. Provide some examples of poor objectives – for example 'To increase sales' or 'To attract more families' – and ask students to rewrite them so that they are SMART.
- Students should discuss and compare the likely objectives of two contrasting travel and tourism providers such as a public organisation and a private organisation. The four mission statements on page 230 of the text might be used as a basis for this discussion.
- The session may be concluded by briefly explaining the format of the external assessment for this unit.

Key words to define

Marketing, marketing objectives, mission statement, vision statement, philosophy of use, SMART.

Answers to textbook activities

Page 229: Students may use the internet to find information for this activity. Possible answers include:

- science and technology – Sellafield Visitor Centre, National Science Museum
- marine life – Sea Life Centres
- pop music – National Centre for Popular Music
- films and television – Bradford's National Museum of Photography, Film and Television
- industry – Black Country Museum, Beamish
- food – Cadbury World.

Page 231: An alternative way of using this activity is as a role play, with students taking the role of interviewer and interviewee.

Build your learning

Students can be asked to find examples of mission statements from local travel or tourism providers and bring their findings to the next session.

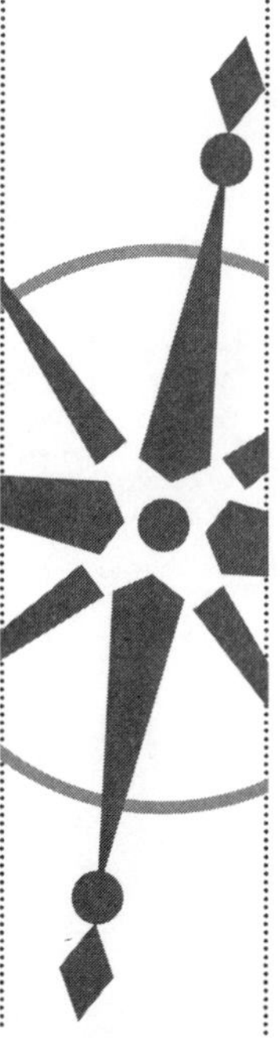

Session 2

Textbook pages 232 to 239

Resources required

- Disneyland case study (on pages 233 and 234 of the textbook
- OHT 2

Objectives of session

- To explore the ways in which organisations analyse the internal (SWOT) and external (PEST) influences on the business environment.

Development of textbook

- A good way of starting this session is to ask students to suggest what factors might affect the success of an organisation. You can list suggestions on the whiteboard in two columns – internal (within the control of the organisation) and external (outside the control of the organisation).
- Using OHT 2, explain how a SWOT analysis is carried out. Students should discuss and identify how SWOT factors may be either positive (strength/opportunity) or negative (weakness/threat). For example, excellent customer service will be a strength, but poor customer service would be a weakness. This should lead to students concluding that an effective SWOT analysis can be of value to an organisation in allowing it to maximise strengths and opportunities while minimising its weaknesses and threats.
- Again using OHT 2, explain how a PEST (or STEP) analysis is carried out. Students can brainstorm a list of factors that might influence travel and tourism providers. Once again, they should understand that factors may have either a positive or negative effect depending on the organisation and the type of products and services offered. To illustrate this point, ask students to discuss which travel and tourism providers would benefit from being located in an area of high unemployment and which would suffer.

Key words to define

Internal factors, SWOT, external factors, market forces, PEST.

Answers to textbook activities

Page 234: Students can work in small groups and present their ideas to the rest of the group. They should be encouraged to interpret the information rather than simply repeat points listed in the case study. For example, entertainment and transport links are a particular strength within the growing business market.

Page 236: Students should identify that technology can be used both as a means of providing a travel or tourism product or service as well as being the actual product or service. For example, computerisation allows holidays and transport to be sold efficiently and technology has provided improved transportation and interactive tourist attractions.

Page 239: Tutors might also like students to consider the impact on the short-break market of the 'money-rich, time-poor' culture that has resulted in many people taking shorter but more frequent holidays. Students can also consider the specific products that have been created to cater for this market such as holiday centres – examples include Center Parc and Oasis – and themed and speciality breaks.

Build your learning

Prior to the next session, students can be asked to read local newspapers and identify any PEST factors that might effect local travel and tourism providers.

Session 3

Textbook pages 239 to 246

Resources required

- Copies of a range of holiday brochures
- OHT 3

Objectives of session

- To identify and analyse the needs and expectations of customers in terms of targeting and positioning travel and tourism products and services.
- To identify and discuss the 'product' element of the marketing mix.

Development of textbook

- This session can be introduced by asking students to consider whether they think it is preferable to create a new product and then find customers to buy it, or to find out what customers want and then create a product that meets these needs. They should understand that the latter option is invariably more successful and is known as a customer-oriented approach.
- You may then explain that the needs and expectations of potential customers greatly influence the way in which different products and services are developed and marketed. This can lead to a general discussion on targeting and positioning products and services. Students can use a range of holiday brochures to compare how products are targeted at different types of customers depending on their needs and expectations. For example, they may review brochures aimed at the elderly market, young adults, families, couples, etc.
- The topic of the marketing mix can be introduced using OHT 3. When discussing product characteristics, students can be asked to identify what they think are the main characteristics of a range of travel and tourism products such as McDonald's, easyJet, Alton Towers, Madame Tussaud's, etc. They might think of five adjectives for each product that sums up the characteristics.
- The power of branding can be demonstrated by asking students to write down the first brand that comes to mind for given generic products. Generic products might include a tour operator, travel agency, theme park, hotel company, museum, airline and restaurant chain. Students can then compare their lists and identify providers that have a strong brand identity.

Key words to define

Customer-oriented approach, unique selling points (USP), customer satisfaction, targeting, positioning, market position, marketing mix, product, goods, services, product characteristics, branding, brand awareness, brand leader, brand extension, brand loyalty.

Answers to textbook activities

Pages 240: For this activity students might also like to consider the ways in which PEST factors may have influenced the rapid growth of budget accommodation. These factors include increases in car ownership and disposable income coupled with the trend to take more short breaks.

Page 244: This activity might be extended by asking students to find out some of the innovative ideas used by Warwick Castle to provide an exciting visitor experience while maintaining its historic image. Information is available on www.warwick-castle. co.uk.

Page 246: Students might identify that the image of Britain could be particularly beneficial in attracting a more mature market that is interested in the historic and cultural aspects of the country. Social classes A and B may also be attracted by the 'civilised' image and have expectations of high standards of accommodation.

Build your learning

Students might investigate one local travel or tourism provider and identify which customers are targeted and what their particular needs and expectations might be.

Session 4

Textbook pages 246 to 251

Resources required

- OHT 3

Objectives of session

- To explain and discuss the ways in which the product life cycle influences the development of travel and tourism products and services.

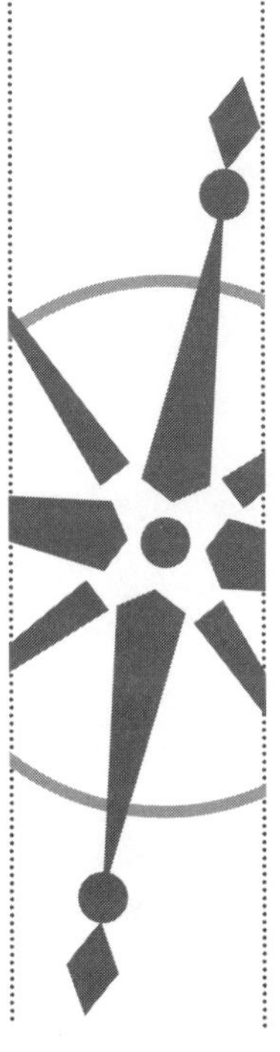

- To evaluate how the location or chain of distribution of travel and tourism products and services forms part of the marketing mix.

Development of textbook

- Students can be reminded of the marketing mix by using OHT 3.
- You might explain that the idea of the product life cycle is based on the notion that all products go through four distinct stages in a similar way that people progress from childhood, young adult, middle age through to old age. Having explained the four stages of the product life cycle, you might ask students to discuss why it is important for an organisation to know where its products lie on the cycle. The discussion should identify that an organisation needs to ensure that it is continually developing new products that will replace its current 'maturity' stage products once they slip into the decline stage.
- Using Figure 4.10 on page 247 of the textbook, students might discuss why the profits are so low in the introduction stage of the product life cycle. Tutors can conclude that many travel and tourism products fail because providers underestimate the huge costs of promoting a new product in this stage.
- When discussing the 'place' element of the marketing mix students need to understand the distinction between location and chain of distribution. Physical location may be important for some providers such as a tourist attraction, but chains of distribution may be of greater concern to other providers such as a tour operator. It is important that students do not fall into the trap of thinking that 'place' for a foreign package holiday is the actual destination (this is clearly part of the product) rather than the location in which the customer buys the holiday. You may clarify this point by asking students to list the possible 'places' for a package holiday. Answers could include travel agency, direct from the tour operator, internet, etc.

Key words to define

Product life cycle, introduction, growth, maturity, decline, place, location, chain of distribution.

Answers to textbook activities

Page 248: Suitable answers for this activity are:

- Southland's museum – decline stage
- Gothic tales – introduction edging into growth stage
- Aqua-experience – maturity but could go into a new growth stage if developments are successful
- Southland's Fayre – growth stage
- Clippers – introduction stage
- Southland's Art Gallery – decline but might be successfully revamped.

Page 250: Students should be careful to avoid the red herrings in this activity.

- Property 1 – The physical accommodation appears highly suitable but students should be able to justify how they will be able to attract sufficient customers given that the area is largely industrial. The usual peak times for people to buy travel products (weekends) are particularly quiet in this area and students need to ask themselves whether customers would go to the area simply to book a holiday.
- Property 2 – Once again the physical accommodation and adjacent parking appears suitable but the first floor location is a serious drawback. It might be suitable once established, but how would Josie be able to attract customers without an eye-catching shop frontage?
- Property 3 – This clearly appears to be the most suitable premises but students need to be wary of the strong competition and the high selling price. A new sole trader might struggle to meet the costs of this location.

Build your learning

Students could be asked to select two or three similar travel or tourism organisations in their area (such as fast food outlets or entertainment venues) and compare them in terms of location. They might consider factors such as transport, passing trade, adjacent facilities, parking, etc.

Session 5

Textbook pages 251 to 255

Resources required

- OHT 3
- Package holiday brochures

Objectives of session

- To explain and discuss how travel and tourism organisations determine price and use pricing policies as part of their marketing mix.

Development of textbook

- It is important that this session begins with a recap on what is meant by the marketing mix, using OHT 3, so that students are aware that this is a continuation of the overall idea of the marketing mix.
- As an introduction to price determination, students may be asked to brainstorm the factors that they think travel and tourism organisations may consider when determining prices for products and services. Case studies on the pricing of mass-market package holidays are helpful in allowing students to see how pricing may be affected by consumer demand and high levels of competition.
- It is useful to encourage students to consider and discuss the impact of the concept of dwell time on price determination. Dwell time might be introduced by prompts such as 'why might you be willing to pay £20 to go to a theme park but only £3 for a visit to a small museum'. The topic might be further developed by asking students to identify how a travel or tourism provider might increase the dwell time to justify a higher entrance charge, by for example the development of factory outlet shopping areas and catering at tourist attractions.
- There are a number of pricing policies that are particularly prevalent in the travel and tourism industry such as discount, variable and seasonal pricing. Students should be encouraged to discuss why such policies are so widely used. Prompts might include 'what types of customers are offered lower prices or discounts at tourist attractions and why', 'can you think of any travel and tourism products that are cheaper at certain times of the day, week or year and why might this happen'. Students could be encouraged to give local examples of different pricing policies.

Key words to define

Price, value for money, breakeven price, dwell time, pricing policy, market penetration pricing, cost-plus pricing, competitive pricing, discount pricing, variable pricing, market skimming strategy.

Answers to textbook activities

Page 252: You may prefer to use actual tour operators' brochures for this activity and extend the costing exercise to include flight supplements, extras, car hire, insurance, etc. If students carry out the activity as a role play, it may also provide evidence for customer service or help to underpin part of the content of some of the optional units.

Page 253: Students should be told that the dwell time quoted for each attraction is the figure estimated by the provider. If they have visited any of the attractions, they might like to consider whether or not it is a realistic figure. They could then discuss the extent to which dwell time is affected by the type of visitor. For example, a family with young children may stay longer at Cadbury's World than two young adults.

Build your learning

Students can be asked to identify how local travel and tourism providers use pricing policies to maintain a competitive advantage. For example, do some offer discounts to certain types of customers or at certain times?

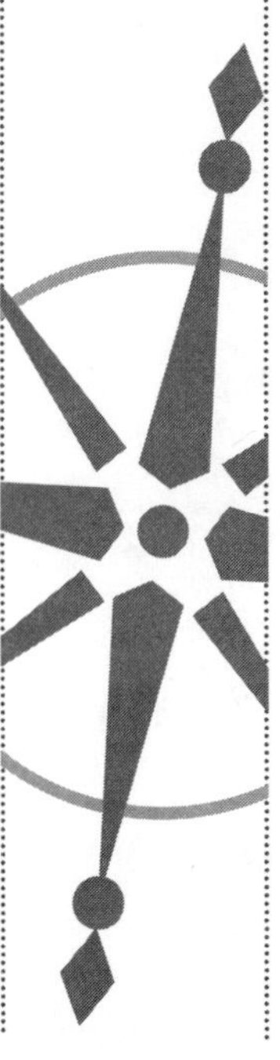

Session 6

Textbook pages 256 to 259

Resources required

- OHT 3

Objectives of session

- To introduce and discuss the general ways in which travel and tourism organisations use promotion as part of their marketing mix.
- To identify how travel and tourism organisations can evaluate the effectiveness of their marketing mix.

Development of textbook

- It is important that this session begins with a recap on what is meant by the marketing mix, using OHT 3, so that students are aware that this is a continuation of the overall idea of the marketing mix. This session is simply an introduction to promotion within the context of the marketing mix and students should be aware that the topic will be covered in greater depth in sessions 10–14.
- Students can develop their understanding of the role of promotion by brainstorming the reasons why they think organisations use promotion. Tutors may clarify their answers using the bullet points on page 256 of the textbook. You may outline, with brief descriptions, the main types of promotion (on page 256 of the text).
- Students need to appreciate that an organisation's marketing mix is continually evaluated and changed when necessary. Ask students to identify examples of when each of the four Ps of the marketing mix might need to be changed. An example would be that pricing policies may change due to a competitor's pricing, decrease in consumer demand, etc.
- It is suggested that at least 30–45 minutes is allowed for the McDonald's case study.

Key words to define

Promotion, promotion mix.

Answers to textbook activities

Page 259: This activity would be greatly enhanced if you are able to organise a group visit to a McDonald's outlet and students have an opportunity to question a member of the management. The member of management might then be invited into the centre to hear students present their findings once they have completed the activity.

Build your learning

In preparation for the further exploration of promotion in sessions 10–14, students can be asked to start collecting examples of travel and tourism promotions that they think are particularly effective. Where space permits, a noticeboard can be used to display the materials.

Session 7

Textbook pages 260 to 266

Resources required

- OHT 4
- Questionnaire from a travel or tourism organisation
- Tour operators' brochures

Objectives of session

- To define market research and its objectives.
- To identify and explain how travel and tourism organisations classify customers into key segments.

Development of textbook

- This session may be introduced by explaining the term market research using the definition on page 260 of the textbook. Students can be asked to discuss and suggest the type of information that travel and tourism organisations might want to find out through market research. Answers can be clarified using the objectives listed on page 260.
- When looking at the objectives of market research it is helpful to link the topic to the marketing mix. For example, ask students to consider what market research information an organisation might want when making decisions on product, price, place and promotion.
- The topic of market segmentation can be introduced by asking students to consider the different ways in which customers can be grouped. OHT 4 can be used to explain the four main types of segmentation. This activity also links to the customer service unit when looking at types of customers.
- Students should be aware that the four methods of market segmentation are frequently used simultaneously by organisations. For example, an organisation might identify target markets that share similar socioeconomic, age, family circumstances and lifestyle characteristics. You might revisit the case study on McDonald's on page 257 and ask students to discuss the market segments that they think McDonald's target. 'Lifestyle' classification is particularly interesting here and should provoke a productive discussion.

Key words to define

Market research, objectives, classifying customers, market segmentation, socioeconomic classification, age, family circumstances, lifestyle segmentation.

Answers to textbook activities

Page 263: You may extend this activity by selecting one of the categories such as social class and asking students to suggest what further market research could be carried out to make the information more useful. An example might be the number, duration and cost of short breaks taken by individuals.

Page 264: Students can consider a wide range of factors in this activity. For example, they may identify that the 16–34 year-old market will age and enter the currently declining 35–44 year-old market. They may consider how the transport provider could maintain the current loyalty of this segment.

Build your learning

Students could investigate a local travel and tourism organisation such as a theatre and identify how the organisation's marketing mix is formulated to attract particular market segments.

Session 8

Textbook pages 266 to 272

Resources required

- OHT 5
- Blank OHTs and pens

Objectives of session

- To explain and discuss how travel and tourism organisations conduct primary research.

Development of textbook

- Using OHT 5, explain the key differences between primary and secondary research.
- Demonstrate the difference between quantitative and qualitative research by asking students a question such as 'do you like going to the theatre'. List the answers on a whiteboard. Then ask 'why do you like/ dislike going to the theatre' and list the answers. Answers to the first question are quantifiable but give no explanation; responses to the second question provide in-depth information but are not quantifiable. The case study on page 272 illustrates the different uses of qualitative and quantitative research.

- The factors to consider when compiling a questionnaire can best be understood by students undertaking the activities on pages 268 to 270. Students should be encouraged to discuss the relative benefits of the three contact methods and suggest suitable uses for each method.
- It is important that students appreciate that when an organisation carries out market research it needs to consider the exercise as part of its overall customer service: the market research activity will influence the respondent's image of the organisation. You might ask students to suggest examples of market research that would create an unfavourable image of the organisation.

Key words to define

Primary market research, field research, qualitative research, quantitative research, surveys, contact methods, observation, focus group.

Answers to textbook activities

Page 268 'Questionnaire layout': The suggested order is 4, 1, 6, 5, 7, 9, 8, 3, 2, 10.

Page 270: It is suggested that students write their questionnaires onto acetates and display them to the rest of the group.

Page 271: Both these activities are time consuming. You may prefer to split the group into two and assign one activity to each group. Both groups should report back to the other group and explain what they found out as well as the strengths and weaknesses of the research method.

Build your learning

Students might write a script for a survey using a telephone contact method. They can role play the interview and evaluate the effectiveness of their questions. They may consider any problems that arose due to the fact that neither party could actually see the other.

Session 9

Textbook pages 273 to 281

Resources required

- OHT 5
- Trade journals

Objectives of session

- To explain and discuss how travel and tourism organisations conduct secondary research.
- To discuss how research findings are analysed and how suitable research techniques are selected.

Development of textbook

- This session can be introduced by recapping on primary and secondary research using OHT 5. Students need to appreciate that market research does not have to be costly to be effective and that most organisations already have a lot of internal secondary information that can be of great value.
- Encourage students to identify some internal sources of secondary information by asking them to suggest how a hotel, for example, could find out information on repeat sales, brand loyalty, seasonality, demand for specific products and services, types of customers using the hotel, customer satisfaction, etc.
- When discussing external sources of secondary information it is useful to provide students with some trade journals such as the *Caterer and Hotelkeeper* and *Travel Weekly*. Students can be given a topic such as 'trends in package holidays' or 'trends in eating out' and use the journals to find relevant information. Analysis of findings provides opportunities to demonstrate key skills in application of number.
- The topic of how to select a suitable research technique can be used to consolidate the main types of primary and secondary market research techniques. Students might be asked to discuss the main advantages and disadvantages of each technique and then identify suitable uses.

Key words to define

Secondary market research, desk research, internal sources, external sources, government publications, trade journals, associations, commercial data, data analysis, survey results, choosing research techniques.

Answers to textbook activities

Page 274: There are a number of possible conclusions that can be drawn from these statistics but students should be wary of relating the figures in one table to those in the other and reaching unfounded conclusions. For example, the increase in self-catering is not necessarily related to the increase in long-haul holidays – in fact it is not, since the majority of long-haul holidays are not self-catering.

Page 275: Once again, there are a number of conclusions that can be drawn. For example, students might suggest that a tour operator should be looking to develop direct or internet booking of short-break holidays.

Page 276: The only statement that is definitely correct is number 2. If students think that statement 4 is correct they should consider that some of the respondents who reported going on holiday on their own or with a friend may still have families even if they did not go on holiday with them!

Page 278: This activity can generate evidence for key skills in application of number.

Page 279: This activity can generate evidence for key skills in communication.

Page 281: Bullet point 1 could be accomplished by internal secondary research and bullet 2 by external secondary research. Bullet 3 might be accomplished through a survey. Bullet 4 might be accomplished through a focus group. Bullet 5 could be accomplished through a combination of external secondary research, survey and focus group.

Build your learning

Students may find it useful to identify what secondary research information is available on the internet. There are a number of valuable websites such as www.staruk.co.uk.

Session 10

Textbook pages 283 to 290

Resources required

- OHT 6

Objectives of session

- To introduce and discuss how marketing communications are used by travel and tourism organisations.
- To discuss the function of advertising within marketing communications.

Development of textbook

- The topic of marketing communications should be introduced by giving an overview of all types of communications using OHT 6. Students should remember that this topic was first discussed in session 6 as part of the marketing mix.
- Students may brainstorm the various objectives that advertising may have before tutors consolidate their ideas using the bullet list on page 283 of the textbook.
- When identifying advertising media, students may be given a scenario and asked to identify the media. For example, 'how would a tourist visiting London for the first time find out about the various tourist attractions in the capital'. You may consolidate using the bullet list on page 283 of the textbook.
- It is important that you spend considerable time discussing the eight types of advertising media. Students might then be asked to list the advantages and disadvantages of each medium on a table.

- Students should also consider how different advertising media are targeted at different market segments. They could, for example, be given a list of magazines, newspapers and commercial television programmes and asked to identify suitable travel and tourism products or services that could be advertised in each medium.

Key words to define

Marketing communications, television, radio, magazines, internet, leaflets, point-of-sale material, posters.

Answers to textbook activities

Page 284: The issue of advertising in Sunday newspapers is important, and students should understand that this is a popular medium for travel and tourism products because readers usually take more time when reading papers at the weekend than they do during the week.

Page 285: Students may generate evidence for application of number in this activity by presenting their findings in graphical or tabular format.

Page 288: You may prefer to incorporate this activity into an organised group visit. It could then also be linked to the customer service material in Unit 5 in terms of the provision of information.

Page 290: This activity can generate evidence for key skills in IT and communication. Students posters can be displayed on a noticeboard.

Build your learning

In preparation for the next session, students should be asked visit a travel agency and collect a minimum of three holiday brochures. To ensure a good range of brochures, such as summer sun, European city breaks, winter sport, long-haul, all-inclusive, youth, etc., you may like to allocate specific types to each student.

Session 11

Textbook pages 290 to 294

Resources required

- OHT 6
- Brochures collected by students

Objectives of session

- To explore how travel and tourism organisations use brochures and direct marketing as an effective part of their marketing communications.

Development of textbook

- Begin this session by recapping on marketing communications generally by using OHT 6. Students need to understand that brochures are one of the main methods of advertising for many travel and tourism products and services. To ensure that students realise that the use of brochures is not limited to holiday companies, they can be asked to identify other travel and tourism organisations that use brochure advertising. Some of the main users are hospitality and catering, transport, conference and event organisers, and tourist attractions.
- It is important for students to understand why brochures are such an effective advertising medium for many travel and tourism products. Ask students to consider whether they would book a foreign package holiday based purely on a press or television advertisement and, if not, why not. Conclusions might include that the choice of holiday is based on detailed information and comparison with other holidays; pricing varies according to factors such as flight times, supplements, etc; customers like to see photographs of various resorts. In essence, brochures (unlike other advertising media) can provide the detailed information that customers require to make an informed decision.

- Students may have a sceptical view of what they perceive as 'junk mail', so Figure 4.32 on page 291 of the textbook can be useful in demonstrating the effectiveness of direct mail. You may like to provide students with the six 'purchasing' media (press, direct mail, leaflets, television, outbound telephone, radio and internet) and ask students to rank them in order of effectiveness before revealing Figure 4.32.
- Students should be asked to consider why direct mail can be so effective. Their responses can provide an opportunity to recap on the importance of targeting specific market segments. You may also develop the link with secondary marketing research at this stage. For example, a suitable prompt question might be 'if a tour operator intended to develop a new European city break destination, how could it use internal secondary research information to produce a direct mailing list'.

Key words to define

Holiday brochures, direct marketing, direct mail, mailshot, mailing lists, telemarketing, door-to-door distribution, media direct response.

Answers to textbook activities

Page 291: This activity will prepare students for the AIDA concept (session 13) and you may like to direct the discussion along these lines. Students can use the brochures that they collected after the last session.

Page 292: This activity can generate evidence for key skills in communication.

Page 294: You may like to link this activity to Unit 5, customer service, and the topic of selling skills. Students could role play the telephone direct marketing script in pairs and evaluate its effectiveness.

Build your learning

In preparation for the next session students could be asked to watch any television holiday or consumer programmes and identify the image that may be created for a travel or tourism provider. You should tell students when suitable programmes are being screened in the coming week.

Session 12

Textbook pages 294 to 302

Resources required

- OHT 6
- Video of television holiday or consumer programme
- Local examples of public relations activities by travel and tourism organisations such as press clippings

Objectives of session

- To explore how travel and tourism organisations use public relations and sales promotions as an effective part of marketing communications.

Development of textbook

- Tutors might begin this session by recapping on marketing communications generally by using OHT 6.
- The topic of public relations can be introduced by asking students to write and then read out their definition of what they believe to be good PR. Consolidate their ideas using the IPR's definition on page 294 of the textbook. You can then ask students to identify all the groups that might make up the 'public' in terms of public relations. Students should be aware that the public does not just refer to an organisation's customers.
- The discussion can be developed by asking students to identify the ways in which organisations can communicate positive PR information to the public. Ideas may be consolidated using the five bullet points on page 294 of the textbook. It is useful to spend some time discussing the link between positive PR and good customer service. A suitable prompt might be 'to what extent might complaint handling, written communication, telephone skills, etc. affect an organisation's public relations image'.

- It is useful to provide students with local examples of PR carried out by travel and tourism organisations. Local newspapers are usually a good source of examples.
- Supermarket chains provide a good starting point for students to identify a range of different sales promotions. Students might discuss how many sales promotion ideas that originated in the retail trade, such as loyalty schemes, special offers, free gifts, have been adopted by the travel and tourism industry.

Key words to define

Public relations, media inclusion, press release, community relations, lobbying, corporate communications, sales promotions, price reductions, free gifts, incentives, special offers, competitions, loyalty incentives, extra products, trade clients.

Answers to textbook activities

Page 295: If a video of a television holiday or consumer programme is available, it can be used for this activity. Alternatively, students can report back from their findings following the 'build your learning' section in the last session. You can expand the activity by asking students to identify particular sections of the public that would be impressed by the media inclusion. For example, television holiday reports from UK seaside resorts often reinforce the traditional, old fashioned image, which may do little to attract youth markets.

Page 296: This activity can generate evidence for key skills in communication.

Page 298: Students should discuss and justify which of the options would provide the greatest media coverage but also target the desired sections of the public. As a yardstick, you might ask students to compare the cost of each PR activity with the expected benefits to the organisation.

Page 300: Sales promotions include free product, special offer and price reductions.

Page 302 'Promoting Pizza Park': Students can choose a number of options for this activity such as designing a competition for local companies or offering a discounted price or extra products for early bookings. You might like to link this activity to the topic of direct marketing by asking students to include a media direct-response section and discuss how responses might be used in future for direct marketing activities.

Build your learning

In preparation for the next session, ask students to look for examples of how different colours are used effectively in marketing communications.

Session 13

Textbook pages 302 to 306

Resources required

- OHT 6
- A range of leaflets from travel and tourism providers

Objectives of session

- To explore how travel and tourism organisations use sponsorship as an effective part of their marketing communications.
- To discuss the ways in which AIDA and timing can affect the overall success of promotions.

Development of textbook

- You might begin this session by recapping on marketing communications generally by using OHT 6.

- The topic of sponsorship can be introduced by asking students to identify examples with which they are familiar. Prompt a group discussion on the benefits of sponsorship to an organisation by, for example, asking students to identify specific sponsorship causes that would create positive PR. Suitable suggestions might include charities, human interest causes, events or voluntary groups, etc. Students might then suggest ways in which a travel and tourism organisation can ensure that its sponsorship is recognised by the public. Ideas might include sponsor's name on all promotional materials, free advertising space (at a sports venue, for example) and T-shirts printed with the sponsor's name.
- If time allows, the topic of AIDA can be developed considerably. Students can use the results from their investigations following the 'build your learning' from the last session to discuss how the use of colour may help with AIDA. You may like to create a further activity by distributing travel and tourism leaflets and asking students to evaluate them in terms of AIDA.
- The topic of promotional timing should also be linked to pricing policies as discussed in session 5. For example, tour operators may promote special offers in December and January to encourage early bookings of summer package holidays and then promote discounted 'late availability' bargains in the early summer months to off-load unsold holidays.

Key words to define

Sponsorship, promotions mix, AIDA, timing.

Answers to textbook activities

Page 302 'Sponsorship': Students should identify that option number 3 is likely to provide the greatest PR coverage, as it will be featured in the local press. This activity may generate evidence for key skills in communication.

Page 304: Since one of Cadbury World's marketing objectives is to 'encourage return visits based on new developments', students might identify that direct mail could be used to inform past customers of any new attractions. They might suggest the content and contact method of the direct mailing.

Page 305: This activity will be greatly enhanced if students are provided with a range of travel and tourism leaflets to evaluate.

Page 306: For this activity students should be careful to distinguish between when customers actually decide to buy a product and when they consume it. For example, people usually book a Christmas package in July or August following their summer holiday. The majority of decisions to join a fitness programme are made in January (following a New Year's resolutions to get fit).

Build your learning

Students can be asked to design a poster or newspaper advertisement based on a given topic and justify their design in terms of AIDA.

Session 14

Textbook pages 306 to 311

Resources required

- Case studies on page 309 of the textbook
- Video of a television consumer programme featuring a travel or tourism organisation

Objectives of session

- To explain and discuss the legal requirements involved in planning and using effective marketing communications.

Development of textbook

- This session requires tutors to explain much detailed information. It may help students to understand the four Acts of Parliament if they are provided with a table to enter their own notes. Suitable column headings might include Act, date, main requirements, impact on the travel and tourism industry.
- For each Act of Parliament, you might explain the details of the first three columns and then ask students to suggest what the likely impacts on the travel and tourism industry might be.
- Students can be encouraged to relate their own experiences of occasions when a travel or tourism product or service has failed to meet the provider's description. The rest of the group might evaluate whether the experience contravened any legal requirements.
- If available, use a video of a television consumer programme featuring a travel or tourism organisation to allow students to discuss which, if any, of the Acts the featured organisation might be contravening.

Key words to define

Legal requirements, Trades Descriptions Act 1968, Package Travel Regulations 1992, Consumer Protection Act 1987, Data Protection Act 1984, regulatory bodies, Independent Television Commission (ITC), Advertising Standards Authority (ASA).

Answers to textbook activities

Page 307: Students might identify that:

- the description of San Antonio is not accurate
- the customer ratings seem suspect given the number of complaints
- there is no mention of the requirement to book a car to qualify for the special offer of 'three weeks for the price of two'
- the description of the hotel is misleading since it suggests that it is small – 'family-run, personal touches' – and the pool and some bedrooms have not yet been refurbished.

Page 309: Students might like to visit the ASA website (www.asa.org.uk) and find more examples of travel or tourism organisations that are featured.

Build your learning

Students have now studied all of the content for this unit. It might be useful for them to recap either by reading through their notes or by reading chapter 4 of the textbook.

Session 15

Resources required

- Sample external assessments from the awarding body
- OHTs 1–6
- List of key words to define from sessions 1–14

Objectives of session

- To prepare for the external unit assessment.

Development of textbook

- This session might be started by revisiting all the 'key words to define' from each of the last 14 sessions. You might achieve this by writing the words on separate slips of paper and creating a team competition, with each team scoring points for giving a correct definition. However, students should be aware that the test will not focus on the meanings of key words and that this activity is simply a useful revision exercise. You may then recap on the key topics by going through the OHTs.
- The remainder of the session should be spent using the sample external assessment materials provided by the awarding body. If the external assessment is based on pre-seen case study material, students should evaluate the material using the topics listed in the specification's 'What you need to learn' section. A number of sessions might need to be arranged to prepare students for external assessment.

The marketing process

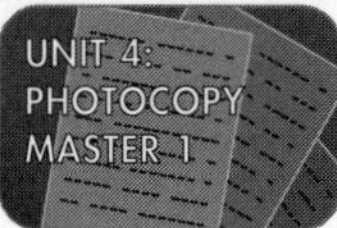

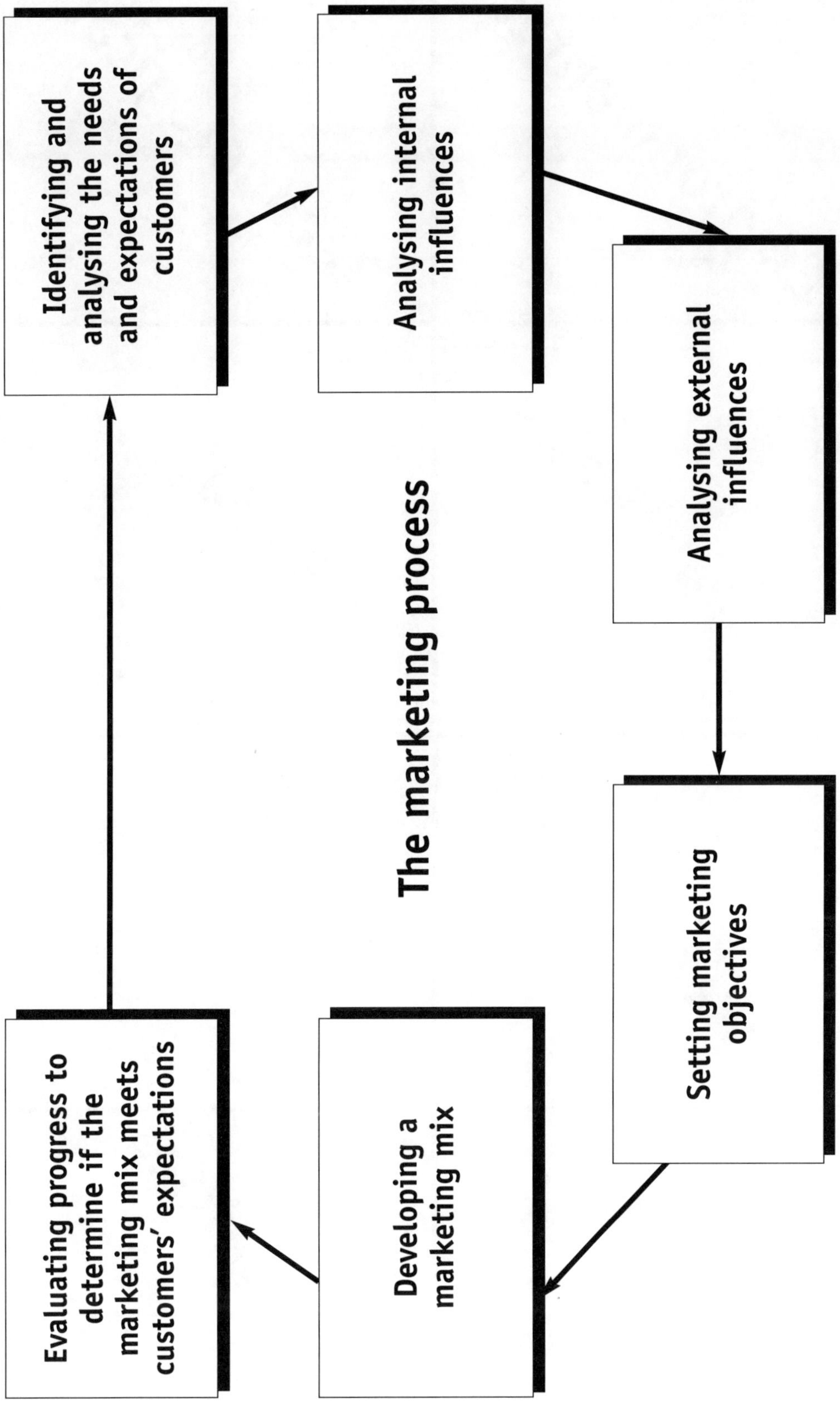

The marketing process

Identifying and analysing the needs and expectations of customers

→ Analysing internal influences

→ Analysing external influences

→ Setting marketing objectives

→ Developing a marketing mix

→ Evaluating progress to determine if the marketing mix meets customers' expectations

→ (back to) Identifying and analysing the needs and expectations of customers

Evaluating the internal and external environments

PEST

Environmental	Technological
Political	Social

SWOT

Weaknesses	Threats
Strengths	Opportunities

The marketing mix

UNIT 4: PHOTOCOPY MASTER 3

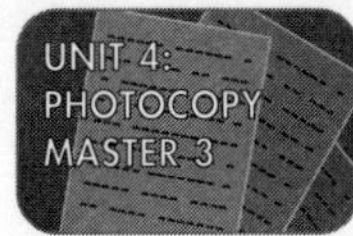

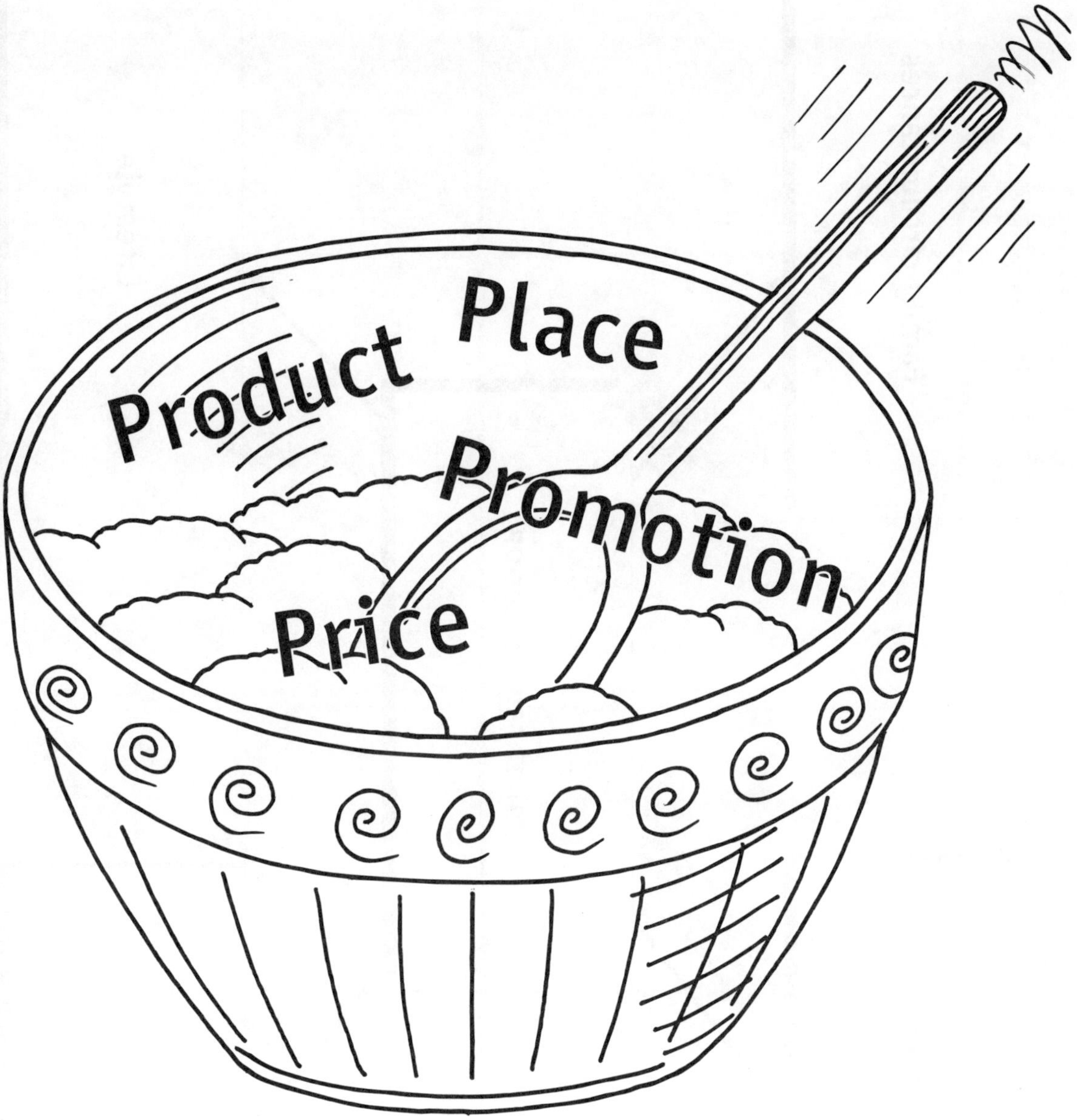

Product
Place
Promotion
Price

UNIT 4: PHOTOCOPY MASTER 4

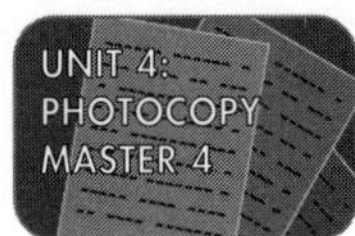

Market segmentation

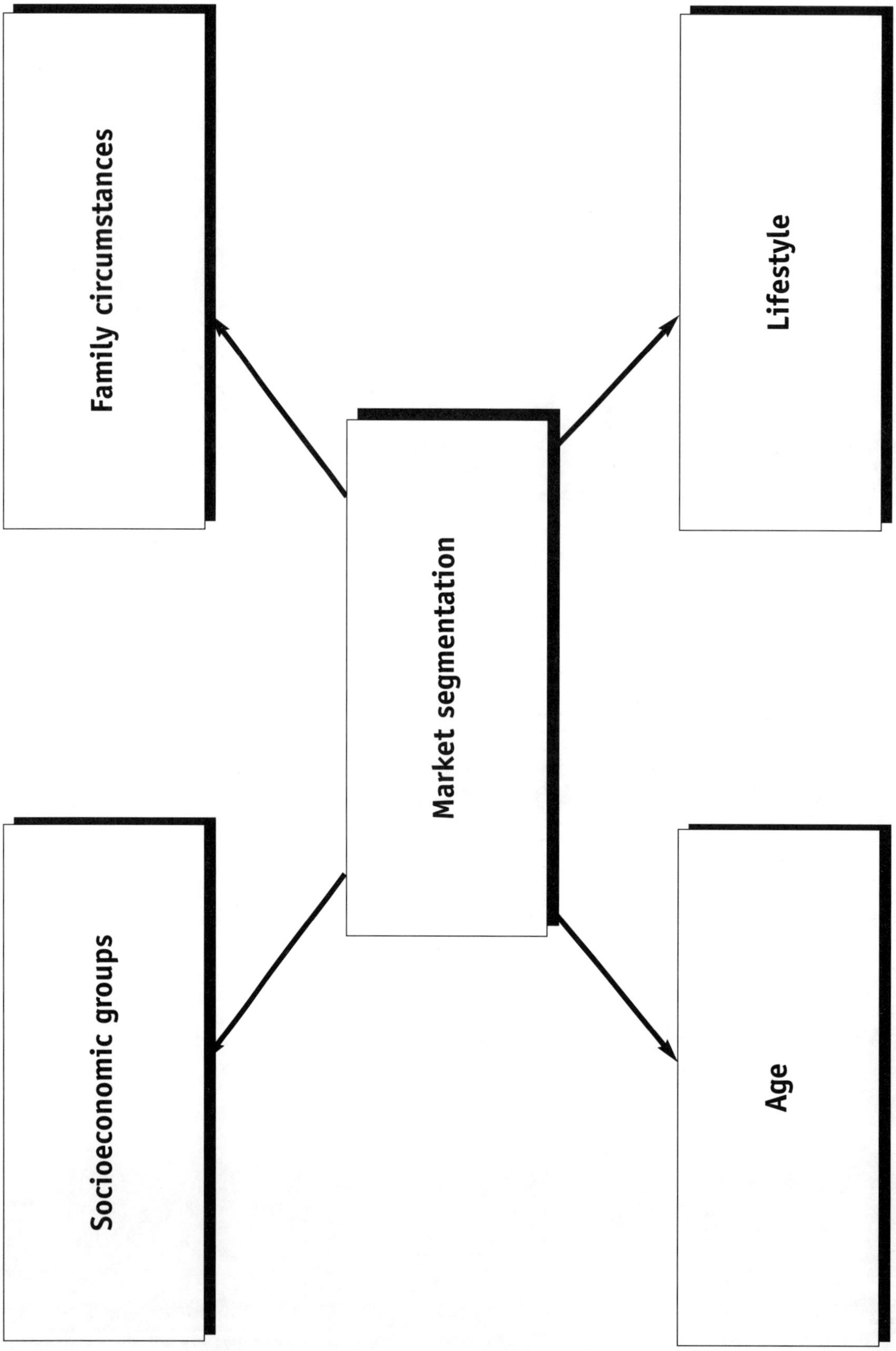
Family circumstances
Lifestyle
Market segmentation
Socioeconomic groups
Age

Market research

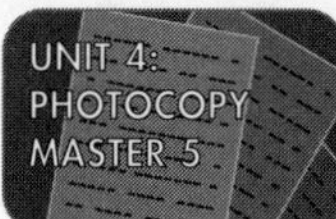

Market research

- **Primary**
  - Surveys
  - Observation
  - Focus groups
- **Secondary**
  - Internal sources
  - External sources

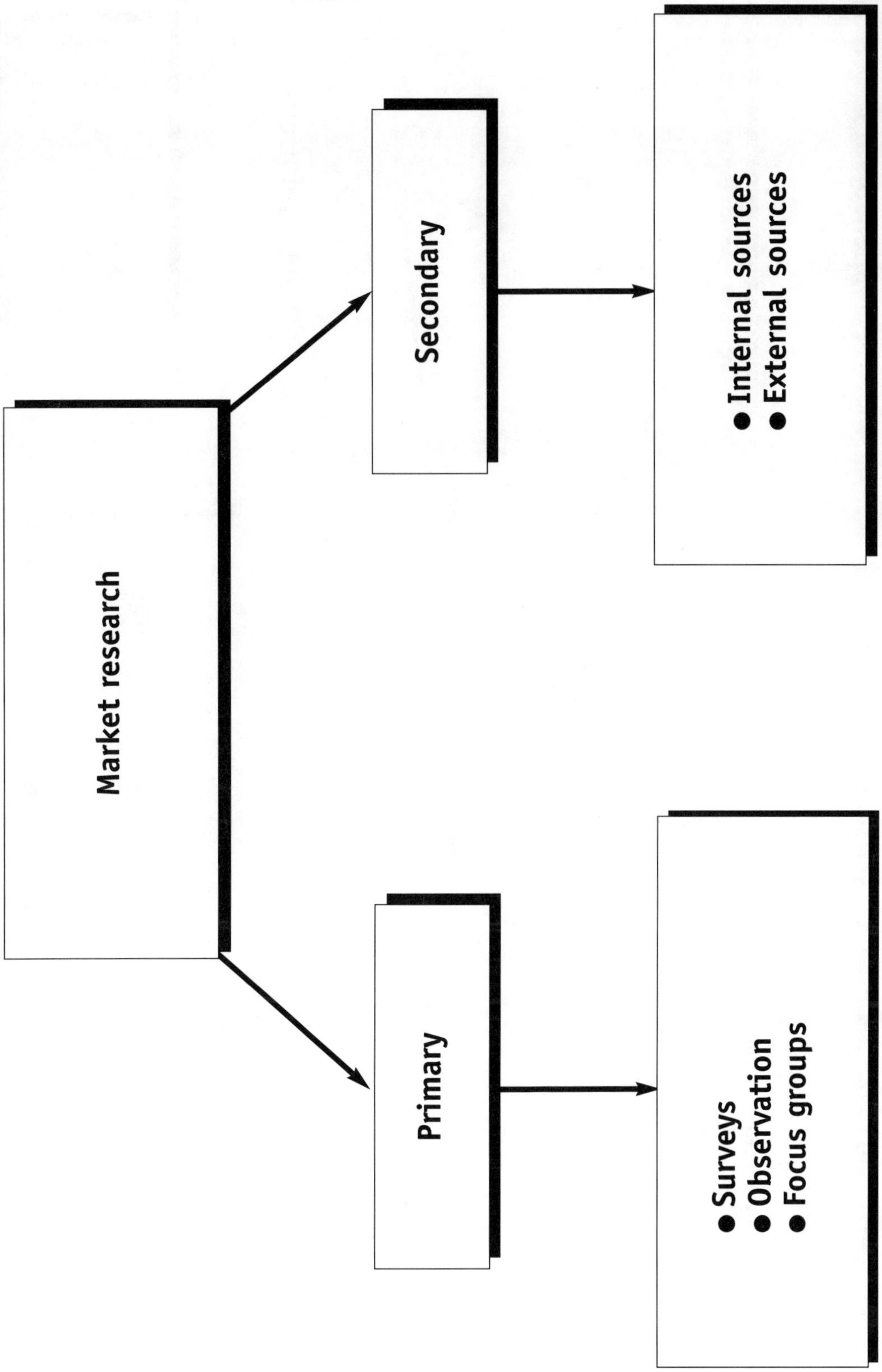

UNIT 4: PHOTOCOPY MASTER 6

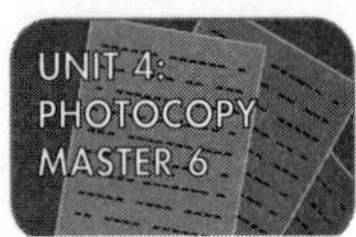

Marketing communications

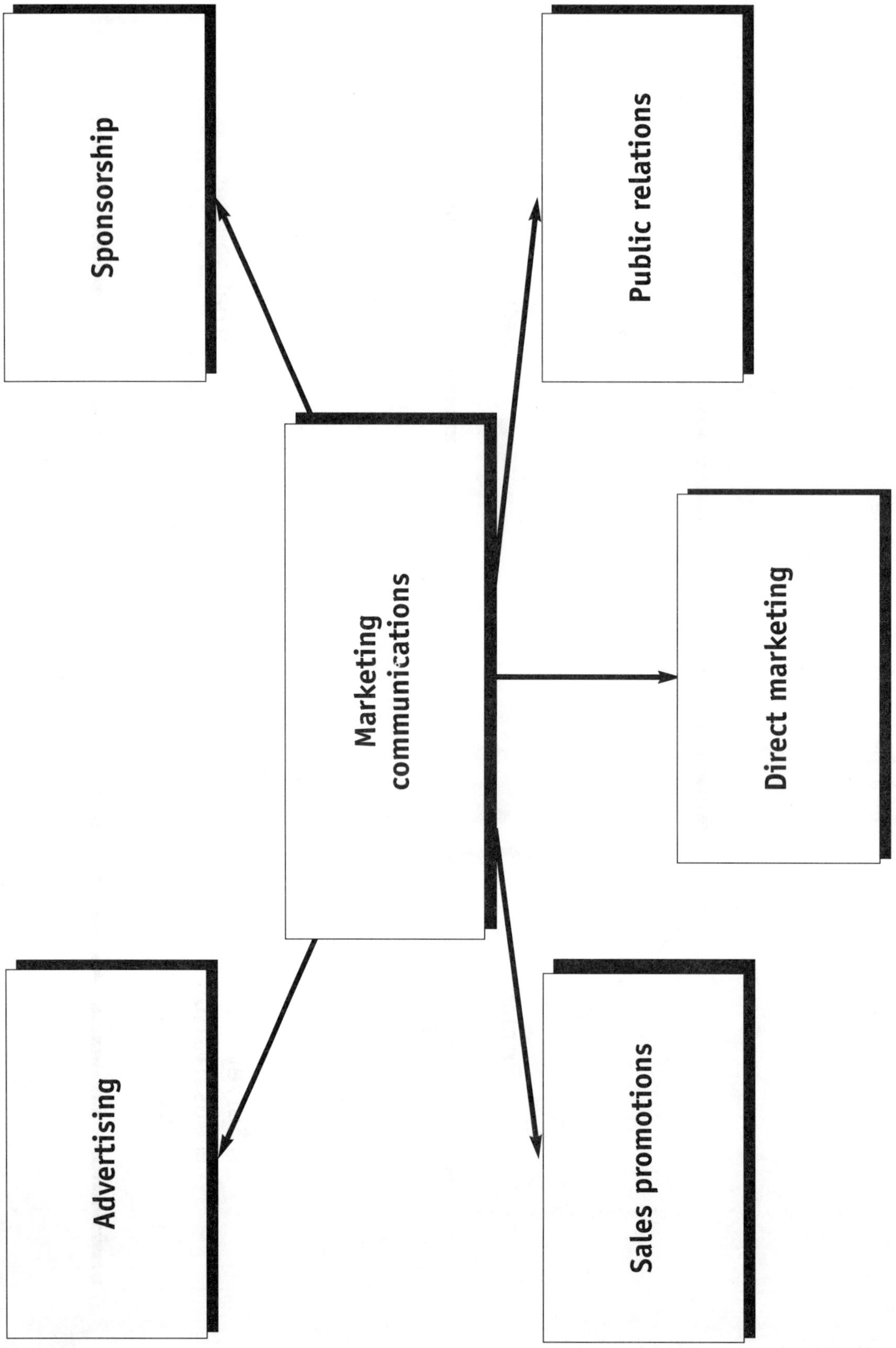

Sponsorship
Public relations
Marketing communications
Direct marketing
Advertising
Sales promotions

Unit 5: Customer service in travel and tourism

Introduction

This unit examines and evaluates the importance of customer service within the travel and tourism industries and the future role that students will play in providing excellent customer service. The unit builds on any knowledge and understanding of the basic skills required in customer service – perhaps acquired during an Intermediate GNVQ qualification in leisure and tourism – and develops students' understanding to incorporate organisational issues involving customer service management.

Delivery suggestions

Theory is important, but this is essentially a 'doing' unit and students need to be provided with a wide range of opportunities to discuss and practise good customer service skills. Throughout the delivery of the unit students should be encouraged to collect examples of both good and bad customer service that they experience for themselves and discuss their examples with the tutor and the group. This should provide numerous opportunities for additional group discussion and help to raise and maintain students' awareness and evaluation of customer service.

Organised group visits are an excellent way of allowing students to evaluate customer service in a range of different providers. Such visits can often serve a dual purpose in allowing students also to collect evidence for another unit such as marketing. For example, a visit to a shopping centre will provide an opportunity to evaluate customer service, but is also a chance to identify and evaluate the promotional materials available.

Links to other units

Unit 1

Customer service has links to the first unit, on investigating travel and tourism, in terms of demonstrating the ways in which the separate components of the industry develop customer service strategies to satisfy the needs of different types of customers.

Unit 4

Students should understand that the 'product' element of the marketing mix often largely comprises of excellent customer service. Students should also understand that the targeting of different market segments might influence the type of customer service offered.

Unit 6

Students can incorporate a customer service element into the internal assessment activity for this unit. The resulting evidence might also be used as evidence for part of the customer service unit.

Unit planner

Session	Session objectives	Text pages
1	To introduce the concept of customer service, in terms of its overall function and importance within the travel and tourism industry To discuss the benefits in terms of increased sales, more customers and improved image To discuss the unit assessment evidence	314 to 319
2	To identify and discuss the importance of customer service in terms of a competitive advantage, happier workforce, satisfied customers and customer loyalty and repeat business	319 to 324
3	To identify and discuss the effects that poor customer service can have	324 to 326
4	To identify and discuss importance of personal presentation in providing excellent customer service	327 to 332
5	To identify and discuss the different types of customer in terms of internal customers, individuals, groups and different ages	333 to 338
6	To identify and discuss the different types of customer in terms of different cultures, non-English speakers and specific needs	338 to 344
7	To discuss the importance of selling skills in providing excellent customer service To discuss the ways in which sales staff can raise customer awareness, establish rapport, identify customer needs, present the product, close a sale and provide after sales service	345 to 350
8	To identify and discuss the ways in which staff deal with customers face-to-face, on the telephone, in writing and verbally	351 to 356
9	To identify and discuss the ways in which staff deal with customers non-verbally To identify and discuss the ways in which staff provide information, give advice and take messages	356 to 362
10	To identify and discuss the ways in which staff deal with customers by keeping records and dealing with problems	362 to 366
11	To identify and discuss how effective complaint handling is an important part of excellent customer service	367 to 373
12	To identify and discuss how travel and tourism organisations assess the quality and effectiveness of customer service using benchmarking and price/value for money, consistency, accuracy and reliability as criteria	374 to 380
13	To identify and discuss how travel and tourism organisations assess the quality and effectiveness of customer service using staffing levels and qualities, enjoyment, health and safety, hygiene, accessibility and individual needs as criteria	381 to 385
14	To discuss the ways in which travel and tourism organisations obtain feedback from staff and customers on the extent to which the organisation's customer service quality standards are being met	385 to 393
15	To consolidate the learning from the previous 14 sessions To discuss and coordinate the assessment evidence for the unit	

Session 1

Textbook pages 314 to 319

Resources required

- OHT 1
- Leaflets and brochures from travel and tourism organisations

Objectives of session

- To introduce the concept of customer service, in terms of its overall function and importance within the travel and tourism industry.
- To discuss the benefits in terms of increased sales, more customers and improved image.
- To discuss the unit assessment evidence.

Development of textbook

- The concept of customer service might be introduced by asking students to draw on their own experiences and suggest what constitutes both good and bad service. Suggestions might be listed on a whiteboard under two columns headed 'good' and 'bad'.
- You can develop these suggestions by emphasising that students' opinions are largely influenced by the ability of staff to identify and meet individual customer's needs and expectations. You can consolidate the discussion by referring students to Figure 5.1 on page 314 of the text.
- You might then ask students to consider and discuss the reasons why customer service is important to travel and tourism organisations. OHT 1 can be used to support the discussion.
- Students need to understand that the end results of good customer service are interdependent. For example, satisfied customers will lead to repeat business, increased sales, better public image, etc.
- The session may be concluded by briefly explaining the format of the assessment for this unit.

Key words to define

Customer service, increased sales, more customers, improved image.

Answers to textbook activities

Page 317 'Selling the benefits of training': Students should identify the key points of the importance of customer service as outlined in OHT 1.

Page 317 'What are your customers worth?': The total amount generated is £357,765. Note that further income will be generated if satisfied customers recommend the organisation to new customers.

Page 318: You may like to substitute the list of travel and tourism providers with local organisations.

Build your learning

Using brochures and leaflets from travel and tourism organisations, students can evaluate how each organisation informs customers about their customer service provision. They might discuss the ways in which this enhances the overall image of the organisation.

Session 2

Textbook pages 319 to 324

Resources required

- OHT 1

Objectives of session

To identify and discuss the importance of customer service in terms of a competitive advantage, happier workforce, satisfied customers and customer loyalty and repeat business.

Development of textbook

- The session might be introduced by recapping on the importance of customer service using OHT 1.
- Students should understand that excellent customer service is frequently the key factor in providing an organisation with a competitive advantage. They might suggest local examples of organisations that have the competitive advantage because of their customer service.
- The benefit of customer service in terms of creating a happier workforce introduces the concept of internal customers as discussed in detail in session 5. Students with work experience might explain how they felt when thanked by customers for providing good service.
- Students should understand the direct link between customer satisfaction and customer loyalty. This topic can also be linked to the marketing unit and the importance of creating brand loyalty and hence repeat business. They can discuss why it is important for travel and tourism organisations to establish loyalty amongst their customers. For example, it is considerably more expensive to attract new customers rather than keeping existing ones. In addition, existing customers are an excellent source of word of mouth recommendation in attracting new customers.

Key words to define

Competitive advantage, happier workforce, customer satisfaction, needs and expectations, customer loyalty, customer retention.

Answers to textbook activities

Page 320: An alternative approach to this activity would be for students to carry out a simple survey of friends and relatives to compare two similar facilities. Results could be presented in the form of graphs and a written report to provide evidence for key skills in communication.

Page 321: Students should identify the importance of effective training to enable staff to feel confident in providing excellent service to customers. In addition, rewarding staff teams for providing excellent service is motivating and creates a team spirit and sense of responsibility.

Page 323: Following the discussion for this activity students might like to write a checklist for a given organisation, such as a travel agency, outlining the key factors in customer service.

Build your learning

Students can investigate the range and level of customer service training provided by local travel and tourism organisations for their staff. They might then suggest ways in which this affects the level of job satisfaction and happiness amongst the workforce. For example, they may discover that a local hotel recruits casual banqueting staff and expects them to work with a minimum amount of training resulting in high labour turnover due to staff feeling that they are undervalued and unable to do their job competently.

Session 3

Textbook pages 324 to 326

Resources required

OHT 2

Objectives of session

To identify and discuss the effects that poor customer service can have.

Development of textbook

- It is useful to begin the session by recapping on the benefits of customer service.
- You can then explain that poor customer service will inevitably result in the reverse of the benefits listed, for example decreased sales, less customers, poor public image, etc. OHT 2 can be used to support this discussion.

- Students might consider how specific aspects of poor customer service can have a negative effect on the organisation. For example, ineffective complaint handling, failure to answer the telephone promptly, giving inaccurate information, poor personal appearance, etc.
- To emphasise the effects of poor customer service students can undertake an extended activity during this session. Working in small groups, they should write their own case study of a fictitious travel or tourism organisation whose customer service is poor. Examples should be given of the ways in which the poor service is manifested. The account should include examples of the negative effects that poor service causes, for example decreased sales, less customers, poor public image, competitive disadvantage, unhappy workforce, dissatisfied customers, and lack of customer loyalty and repeat business. Once the case studies are completed, students can read them out to the other groups and discuss the various features that typify poor customer service.

Key words to define

Effects of poor service, decreased sales, less customers, poor public image, competitive disadvantage, unhappy workforce, dissatisfied customers, customer disloyalty, lack of repeat business.

Answers to textbook activities

Page 324: The discussion for this activity might highlight the fact that certain types of customers may be treated less favourably than other types. For example, young people/students may comment that they feel they are not treated as well as older customers and consider the reasons why this might be. They may then identify that the young customer of today soon becomes the mature customer of tomorrow. Therefore, if they experience poor service when young they may never return. The discussion should reach the conclusion that all customers have the right to expect the same high level of service.

Page 326: The end of section activity may be accomplished by two organised group visits. On each visit it would be helpful if a member of the organisation agrees to speak to the students and answers their questions. Their findings can be used for the unit assessment evidence.

Build your learning

In preparation for the next session, students should be asked to visit a number of local travel and tourism organisations and record their first impressions of the staff. The type of issues that they might be asked to look at should include the appearance and uniforms of staff, personal hygiene and the ways in which the personality and attitude of the staff affected their overall first impression.

Session 4

Textbook pages 327 to 332

Resources required

- Mail order catalogues featuring a wide range of clothing

Objectives of session

- To identify and discuss the importance of personal presentation in providing excellent customer service.

Development of textbook

- This session might start by linking the build your learning from the previous session with the activity on page 327. Suggestions from students can be listed on a whiteboard in four columns. The column headings of 'dress', 'personal hygiene', 'personality' and 'attitude' can be added at the end.
- When discussing 'dress', students should explore the different impressions that dress can create and the reasons why different organisations have different dress codes. They should understand that there is no single correct type of dress, as it will vary according to the needs and expectations of customers of the individual organisations. They might identify and compare travel and tourism organisations who create either a formal of informal impression through the way in which staff are dressed.

- Students should take some time exploring the ways in which attitude and personality requirements may differ according to the situation and type of customer. For example, customers who may prefer a less formal attitude and situations where greater formality is called for. They should understand that they may need to modify their attitude and behaviour towards individual customers and it is vital that they develop an ability to identify and understand the appropriate behaviour in any given situation.

Key words to define

Personal presentation, first impression, dress and appearance, uniform, personal hygiene, personality, attitude.

Answers to textbook activities

Page 328 'Uniform': Students may present their ideas to the rest of the group, justifying their choice. At the end of the presentations the whole group can discuss which of the ideas are the best.

Page 328 'Personal hygiene': This activity can be extended by asking students to draw up a 'personal hygiene' checklist. You should emphasise the fact that staff who smoke should always ensure that they do not smell of cigarettes when dealing with customers.

Page 329: Suitable personality traits might include being organised, smartly dressed, flexible, confident, outgoing, etc.

Page 331: If students are also studying optional language units they might like to conduct the role plays with the customer speaking in a foreign language.

Build your learning

Students might investigate the specific dress and hygiene requirements in jobs where health, safety and hygiene are a prime consideration.

Session 5

Textbook pages 333 to 338

Resources required

- OHT 3

Objectives of session

- To identify and discuss the different types of customers in terms of internal customers, individuals, groups and different ages.

Development of textbook

- This session might be started by asking students to brainstorm all of the different types of customers who use travel and tourism organisations. Ideas can be consolidated by using OHT 3.
- The concept of internal customers was introduced in session 2, when the importance of customer service in creating a happier workforce was discussed. Students should be encouraged to draw on their own experiences to identify how good internal customer service can improve both the working environment and the service that is offered to external customers. They might relate examples of both good and poor internal customer service and explain the effect that it had on them and their colleagues.
- When discussing the differences between individual customers and groups, students should understand that all customers like to feel that they are viewed as an individual by the organisation and its staff. Therefore, even if they are part of a large group, staff should endeavour to show that their individual needs are important and met. You might use an example, such as the group welcome meeting that resort representatives hold at the beginning of a package holiday, and ask students to consider how the representative can ensure that each holidaymaker feels that they are important as an individual.

- The issue of dealing with customers of different ages might be developed by referring back to the last session and the ways in which attitude and behaviour differs according to the type of customer. For example, staff may adopt a less formal attitude with children and young adults than older customers. However, students should understand that stereotyping customers according to their age is not good customer service practice and liable to offend.

Key words to define
Internal customers, colleagues, management and supervisors, staff teams, employees, staff in other functional departments or organisations, external customers, individuals, groups, people of different ages.

Answers to textbook activities
Page 334: This activity might be extended by asking students to interview a member of staff in a travel or tourism organisation and identify all of their internal customers. Students' findings can be reported back to the group.

Page 335: In suggesting further ways in which passengers can be treated well, students may like to draw on their own experiences of travelling on public transport and identify examples of good and bad practice.

Page 338: In the feedback session following this activity, you should emphasise the problems incurred through stereotyping age categories.

Build your learning
The topic of types of customers can be linked to market segmentation as covered in the marketing unit. Students might like to use some of the market segments that they identified in activities in the marketing sessions and suggest how their customer service requirements might vary.

Session 6
Textbook pages 338 to 344

Resources required
- OHT 3

Objectives of session
- To identify and discuss the different types of customer in terms of different cultures, non-English speakers and specific needs.

Development of textbook
- This session should be started by reminding students of different types of customers using OHT 3. The topic of culture can be introduced by asking students to define the term. It is a very difficult term to define concisely. You may help students' understanding by asking them to suggest anything that they would associate with US culture and developing a discussion on the ways in which US culture may have influenced the level of service that we expect.
- When discussing non-English speaking customers, students may draw on their own experiences of travelling abroad and suggest some of the problems that they experienced. Ideas can be listed on a whiteboard and then discussed as to how such problems might be resolved through excellent customer service.
- 'Specific needs' is a sensitive topic and requires careful handling to avoid stereotyping. Students might be asked to suggest what they understand by the term and list examples of specific needs. You should be careful to emphasise that most customers will have specific needs at some time and that it is a member of staff's responsibility to identify their needs and react in an appropriate way. It is vital that students fully understand that if a customer's needs are different the member of staff should act in such a way that makes the customer feel different.

Key words to define

Different cultures, cultural background, non-English speakers, specific needs, Disability Discrimination Act 1995.

Answers to textbook activities

Page 342: The second part of this activity is particularly suited to an organised group visit. You might select a destination that pays close attention to the specific needs of customers so that students can observe and evaluate good practice. Suitable destinations might include national chains of travel or tourism providers, multi-facility leisure centres or large shopping malls, such as Meadowhall.

Page 343: As with all role-play activities it is preferable to ensure that the role-play environment is as realistic as possible. You should therefore give some consideration to how the room is set up, the use of furniture, etc. Rather than role play each scenario in front of the group, it may be preferable to video record individual role plays and play them back to the rest of the group for evaluation.

Build your learning

In preparation for the next session, students can be asked to visit any organisation in which staff are in a selling situation and identify what is good and poor about the way in which they sell the organisation's products and services.

Session 7

Textbook pages 345 to 350

Resources required

- OHT 4
- A selection of holiday brochures

Objectives of session

- To discuss the importance of selling skills in providing excellent customer service.
- To discuss the ways in which sales staff can raise customer awareness, establish rapport, identify customer needs, present the product, close a sale and provide after sales service.

Development of textbook

- This session might start by asking students to identify and discuss why selling skills are an important part of excellent customer service. Students should understand clearly that while selling a product is important in terms of increased sales, identifying and satisfying customers' needs is of greater importance in a selling situation.
- Students can be asked to consider the specific qualities that are needed in a selling situation. The discussion can be consolidated by using the qualities in the bullet list on page 345 of the textbook and OHT 4. You might relate this to the discussion from session 4 when students considered the personality and attitude needed to provide excellent customer service.
- In dealing with the topics of establishing rapport and identifying customers' needs, you might introduce the importance of good communication and effective questioning techniques.
- Students can be asked to identify and discuss specific travel and tourism products where after-sales service is particularly important. Consider, for example, the service that a travel agent provides after the customer has booked and paid for a package holiday.
- If students completed the 'build your learning' activity suggested in the last session, they might like to evaluate the selling skills of the staff that they met in terms of AIDA criteria.

Key words to define

Selling skills, raising customer awareness, establishing rapport, identifying customer needs, presenting the product, closing the sale, after-sales service.

Answers to textbook activities

Page 347: You might provide students with a selection of holiday brochures so that they can select a holiday for the customer on the basis of the customer's responses to the questionnaire.

Page 348 and 349: These activities can be used for the unit assessment evidence. The activity on page 349 would be improved if students prepared for the role play on Tunisia by looking through some holiday brochures and familiarising themselves with Tunisia as a holiday destination.

Build your learning

You can arrange for a member of staff from a local travel or tourism provider to talk to students about the importance of selling skills for their staff. An organisation such as a national travel agency, that carries out formal sales training with its staff would be ideal.

Session 8

Textbook pages 351 to 356

Resources required

- Examples of written communications

Objectives of session

To identify and discuss the ways in which staff deal with customers face-to-face, on the telephone, in writing and verbally.

Development of textbook

- This session can be started by asking students to define the term communication. It is important they understand that it is a two-way process, with information being both sent and received between customers and staff. They can then discuss the factors that help communication flow such as attitude of staff, effective questioning and response to questions, etc.
- Students might be asked to discuss which they find easiest and why: face-to-face, written or telephone communication. This can then be expanded into a discussion on the main advantages and disadvantages of each method of communication. The discussion can be summarised by entering the advantages and disadvantages in a table.
- The topic of written communication may be explored further by asking students with part-time jobs to explain the ways in which their employers communicate in writing with their customers. You might provide students with a selection of written communications to evaluate, such as letters, faxes, menus and leaflets. Students should be aware that written communication is not just paper-based but includes communications on display boards, computers, etc.

Key words to define

Dealing with customers, face-to-face communication, telephone communication, written communication, verbal communication.

Answers to textbook activities

Page 351: Students can use a lot of imagination for this activity. The important learning outcome is that students identify the needs of the particular type of customer and communicate in an appropriate manner.

Page 352: In preparation for this activity, students could first design a suitable telephone message pad to use in the role plays.

Page 353: This activity can provide evidence for the key skill IT if students word process their letter. They could also design and add a letterhead and logo to the letter.

Build your learning

In preparation for the next session, briefly define what is meant by body language and ask students to identify, before the next session, five occasions when someone communicated something to them using body rather than verbal language.

Session 9

Textbook pages 356 to 362

Resources required

- Photographs of people taken from a magazine

Objectives of session

- To identify and discuss the ways in which staff deal with customers non-verbally.
- To identify and discuss the ways in which staff provide information, give advice and take messages.

Development of textbook

- This session might start by asking students to report back on their findings from the 'build your learning' activity in session 8. You might also provide magazine photographs of people and ask students to evaluate the body language of each. The key features of body language can be listed on the whiteboard in two columns – 'open body language' and 'closed body language'.
- When discussing the role of staff in providing information and giving advice, it is important that students understand the need for absolute accuracy and objectivity when providing product information. You might emphasise this point by providing students with some 'what if' scenarios. For example, what if a member of staff provides the wrong information on train times or advises a customer that a PG certificate film is suitable for very young children?
- Students should understand that taking and relaying messages usually involves a combination of written, face-to-face and/or telephone communication. It is important that they identify and discuss all the information that needs to be recorded when taking a message. You can ask them to suggest why each item of information is needed. For example, the name of the person taking the message should be recorded in case there is any query about the message later.

Key words to define

Non-verbal communication, body language, open body language, closed body language, providing information, giving advice, taking and relaying messages.

Answers to textbook activities

Page 357: This activity can provide evidence for the key skill IT if students use the internet to complete it.

Page 358: At the end of this activity, you might remind students that work colleagues can often be the quickest and most effective source of information.

Page 360: Students should avoid the pitfall of making the advice to customers too complicated. At the end of the activity they might discuss as a group how effective such a system would be in meeting customers' needs and any possible drawbacks.

Page 362: This activity can provide evidence for the key skill IT if the students' designs use a computer.

Build your learning

In preparation for the next session students can be asked to think about, and make a list of, all of the records that a travel and tourism organisation might keep on its customers. They might consider records kept on customer details, financial transactions, health, safety and security, complaints, etc.

Session 10

Textbook pages 362 to 366

Resources required

- Examples of some customer records from travel or tourism organisations
- Holiday brochures that feature Portugal

Objectives of session

- To identify and discuss the ways in which staff deal with customers by keeping records and dealing with problems.

Development of textbook

- This session might be introduced by asking students to report back on some of the customer records that they have thought of, following the 'build your learning' section in session 9. Ideas can be listed on a whiteboard and students asked to discuss why each type of record is important to the organisation, its staff and the customer.
- Students would benefit from evaluating some real examples of travel and tourism records and identifying the sort of information that is included. Suitable examples might include hotel registration cards, booking forms, bills, etc.
- The topic of providing assistance can help to recap on discussions in session 6 dealing with customers with specific needs. Students might identify a range of specific needs that customers have and suggest the type of assistance that they may require. For example, a mother with an infant may need to access changing facilities, bottle warming facilities, etc., or require assistance manoeuvring a pushchair.
- When discussing how staff deal with customers' problems, it is important that students understand the need to evaluate the gravity of the problem and seek assistance if necessary. For example, a customer who has collapsed will need immediate first aid attention and an inexperienced member of staff should not delay in seeking help.
- Students should appreciate the importance of being vigilant and observant so that they can quickly identify when a customer needs assistance or has a problem that needs resolving. They might suggest ways in which this can be achieved, such as observing the body language and behaviour of customers as well as listening carefully to what they say.

Key words to define

Keeping customer records, providing assistance, dealing with problems.

Answers to textbook activities

Page 363: This activity can be used to recap on session 7 and selling skills.

Page 364: Students may not know the correct procedure for some of these situations so it is worth spending some time discussing the correct answers with them. For example, explaining the procedure that all customers need to go through when they have lost their credit cards.

Page 364: For this activity students should identify that they are dealing with two customers: the lost person and the customer who has lost a relative. Each customer will have different needs that have to be met. They might compare the different needs in each scenario. For example, there will be a more pressing need for urgency and drastic action in the case of the young child than there will be in the case of the teenager.

Build your learning

Students can investigate a travel or tourism provider and identify what formalised procedures are in place for dealing with specific customer problems, such as lost belongings or a lost child.

Session 11

Textbook pages 367 to 373

Resources required

- OHT 5
- OHT 1

Objectives of session

- To discuss how effective complaint handling is an important part of excellent customer service.

Development of textbook

- This session might be introduced by asking students to consider what they think most customers expect and want to happen when they make a complaint. Their suggestions can be consolidated by using Newcastle's complaint policy on page 367 of the textbook.
- You can expand this discussion by outlining the four types of complainer given on pages 368 and 369 of the textbook and asking students to consider what each type of complainer might want. Students should conclude that different customers will expect different outcomes to their complaint. You should then explain that there are certain steps that should be taken when dealing with all complaints. OHT 5 can be used to explain these steps.
- It is worth spending some time looking at the effects that poor complaint handling can have. Students can relate examples of when they have been dissatisfied with the way in which a complaint has been dealt with and explain the effect that this had on their image of the company and likelihood of using it again. You might use OHT 1 from session 1 and ask students to identify the negative effects that poor complaint handling would have on each factor.
- The session should be concluded by reinforcing the point that members of staff should always call a supervisor for help if they feel unable to handle a complaint on their own. Students might suggest examples of complaint handling situations that they would feel uneasy about handling alone.

Key words to define

Handling complaints, complaints procedure, aggressive complainers, passive complainers, constructive complainers, professional complainers, dealing with complaints, deciding on action.

Answers to textbook activities

Page 370:

1. 'Duly note' suggests lack of interest. A more suitable phrase might be 'I was most concerned to note.'
2. This is clearly a ludicrous argument. If it is true, an organisation as large as the Disney Corporation would be unable to sustain its reputation for excellent customer service.
3. To suggest that a customer is 'hypercritical' attempts to shift the blame for the situation onto the customer – a very poor and counter-productive approach to complaint handling.
4. The entrance price paid is irrelevant – all customers should be able to expect and receive the same high level of customer service.
5. Highly unlikely!

Page 371/2: Many problems could have been resolved if the representative had given better information, identified the main needs of her customers and ensured that the service provided was effective in meeting these needs. Poor communication was at the root of most problems and could easily have been avoided.

Build your learning

Many organisations have a standardised letter that they send out immediately to a customer's written letter of complaint, stating that they are very concerned about the matter, investigating it fully and will contact the complainant soon regarding the complaint. Ask students to draft such a letter and explain why travel and tourism organisations may use it as part of their complaint handling procedure.

Session 12

Textbook pages 374 to 380

Resources required

- OHT 6

Objectives of session

- To identify and discuss how travel and tourism organisations assess the quality and effectiveness of customer service using benchmarking and price/value for money, consistency, accuracy and reliability as criteria.

Development of textbook

- This session can be introduced by asking students to consider why it might be important for travel and tourism organisations to assess the quality and effectiveness of their customer service. Suitable responses will include the confirmation that customers' needs and expectations are being met and that the organisation retains a competitive advantage.
- The discussion can be further developed by asking students to consider what the likely results would be if an organisation did not assess the quality and effectiveness of their customer service.
- You will need to explain in detail the concept of benchmarking and how it may be used in the travel and tourism industry. Students may be able to give examples of benchmarks that they are familiar with, such as the compensation offered by rail companies for delayed journeys.
- Students might be asked to suggest what general criteria travel and tourism organisations could use to assess the quality and effectiveness of their customer service. Ideas can be listed on a whiteboard and consolidated using OHT 6.
- Discussions on the quality criteria of 'value for money' can be linked to the marketing unit and decisions on pricing policies and dwell time (where appropriate).
- The topic of consistency, accuracy and reliability can be reinforced by emphasising that an organisation's reputation for customer service is based on its 'weakest link'. For example, a customer may have experienced excellent service on nine visits but if on the tenth visit the service is poor, this will be the 'benchmark' that the customer remembers.

Key words to define

Assessing quality, benchmarking, value for money, consistency, accuracy, reliability.

Answers to textbook activities

Page 376: For this activity, students will usually focus on the hotels that are the lowest/highest scorers and the quality criteria that score the highest/lowest. However they should not ignore the 'middle' scorers, for these may well be the areas in which problems are easiest to remedy in the first instance. Students may like to suggest what the company should do with the information. For example, the bar manager from the Coventry hotel might liaise with the Oxford hotel's bar manager on ways in which service could be improved. Alternatively, the group customer service manager could investigate why the quality of the reservations systems at Bath and Cardiff are so good and set benchmarks of a similar standard for the rest of the company.

Page 377: The criteria that students might identify as being directly related to customer service delivery are:

- staff attentiveness and efficiency
- efficiency and simplicity of booking service
- speed and efficiency of check-in/out.

Page 378: This activity can be extended by providing students with fare classes from other transport providers, such as rail or ferry companies, and asking them to carry out similar activities.

Page 380: For this activity students should be reminded of previous sessions that have dealt with identifying and satisfying the general and specific needs of customers.

Build your learning

Following the activity on page 378, ask students to find one example of a travel or tourism provider who offers a range of different levels of service, according to the amount that the customer pays. A typical example might be a provider such as Center Parcs or Oasis.

Session 13

Textbook pages 381 to 385

Resources required

- OHT 6

Objectives of session

- To identify and discuss how travel and tourism organisations assess the quality and effectiveness of customer service using staffing levels and qualities, enjoyment, health and safety, hygiene, accessibility and individual needs as criteria.

Development of textbook

- This session can be introduced by using OHT 6 to recap on the criteria that travel and tourism organisations employ to assess the quality and effectiveness of their customer service.
- When discussing staffing levels, students should understand the distinction between being understaffed resulting in poor customer service and being overstaffed resulting in low profitability. You might ask students to consider some of the difficulties in predicting suitable staffing levels in certain travel and tourism situations: an example might be the unexpected coach party turning up during a quiet period.
- Students need to fully appreciate that health and safety factors are always a key quality criterion and take precedence over all others. You may illustrate this by giving an example, such as the customers whose 'enjoyment' (another quality criterion) of a hotel stay might be dampened by a fire evacuation in the middle of the night.
- The topic of hygiene can be linked to the discussions on personal presentation in session 4.
- Students can be asked to brainstorm all the ways in which an organisation ensures that its services are accessible and available to customers. Responses might include opening hours, directions on how to reach the organisation, ease of making reservations, access for those with specific needs such as mobility impairment, etc.
- Students should consider the relationship between setting quality standards while also meeting individual customer needs. They should conclude that quality standards set the benchmark, but that there should be sufficient flexibility to offer more when required. The hamburger example on page 385 is a good example of this point.

Key words to define

Staffing levels and qualities, enjoyment, health and safety, hygiene, accessibility, availability, individual needs.

Answers to textbook activities

Page 381: The key points that students might identify are:

- poor advance information and staff knowledge
- inadequate staffing levels
- inappropriate staff attitudes
- failure to respond quickly to customer's needs.

Page 384: This section would cover issues such as ensuring children are supervised at all times, safety guidelines on beaches and at swimming pools, ensuring children are protected from the sun, what to do in the event of illness, safety advice on the use of lifts and accommodation balconies, etc.

Page 385: You might like to arrange a group visit to enable students brainstorm the quality criteria for a specific travel or tourism organisation.

Build your learning

In preparation for the next session, students can be asked to find one example of how a travel or tourism organisation obtains feedback on the extent to which their quality standards are being met.

Session 14

Textbook pages 385 to 393

Resources required

- Examples of customer feedback forms

Objectives of session

- To discuss the ways in which travel and tourism organisations obtain feedback from staff and customers on the extent to which the organisation's customer service quality standards are being met.

Development of textbook

- If students have undertaken the 'build your learning' in session 13, you can ask them to identify ways in which organisations obtain feedback on their customer service quality. Suggestions can be listed on the whiteboard before outlining the six main methods in the specification.
- It is useful to provide some examples of feedback forms for students to read and evaluate, such as questionnaires from tourist attractions or restaurants.
- When discussing informal feedback from staff, you can recap on the importance of internal customer service as discussed in session 5. You might ask students to consider why it is important for staff to be encouraged to discuss feedback that they have received from their customers and how this contributes to a happier workforce, increased job satisfaction and, ultimately, better customer service.
- The topic of formal feedback methods can be linked to marketing research, which is covered in Unit 4.

Key words to define

Feedback techniques, informal feedback, formal feedback, suggestion boxes, focus groups, mystery shoppers, observation, customer comment books, evaluating quality criteria.

Answers to textbook activities

Page 386: This activity includes examples of all of the six feedback methods and students should be able to identify each. As an extension to the activity, you might ask students to evaluate which of the feedback information they consider to be the most reliable and, therefore, most useful. For example, if feedback is informal from customers, it would need to be established whether this was a widely held opinion or simply an off-the-cuff remark from a single customer.

Page 388: This activity can provide evidence for the key skill IT if the comment card is word-processed.

Page 389: Students should identify that some aspects of customer service are outside the parameters of quality standards, such as unacceptable weather and the temporary unavailability of facilities. They need to understand that feedback from customers should be viewed within the context of the situation at the time of the feedback.

Page 390: With the agreement of a travel or tourism provider, you might arrange for students to carry out a 'mystery visitor' exercise in a real organisation. A suitable venue might be an out-of-town shopping mall.

Page 392: This activity can provide evidence for all three core key skills if the report is word-processed and students use numerical calculations and representations in their report.

Build your learning

In preparation for the final session, students should be asked to review all of the information that they have collected during the last 14 sessions. This should include class notes, answers to activities, information gathered from organised visits and any other information that they have collected.

Session 15

Resources required

- Handout of portfolio assessment for the unit

Objectives of session

- To consolidate the learning from the previous 14 sessions.
- To discuss and coordinate the assessment evidence for the unit.

Development of textbook

- This session might be introduced by recapping on the key words that have been defined and used throughout this unit. You might like to create a short quiz and ask student teams to define a selection of the key words given in each session.
- Following the 'build your learning' activity from session 14, you might then ask students to brainstorm examples of good customer service practice in travel and tourism organisations. You should guide the discussion to ensure that a range of examples are found for all the unit subheadings:
  - why excellent customer service is important
  - personal presentation
  - types of customers
  - dealing with customers
  - handling complaints
  - assessing the quality and effectiveness of customer service.

- You will need to spend some time explaining what the unit assessment evidence requirements are and how grades are decided.
- For part one of the assessment, students can use personal evidence from part-time jobs or work placement. Alternatively, the evidence can be generated through role-play sessions. Suitable role plays from the textbook can be found on pages 331, 343, 347, 348, 349, 351, 352, 353, 356, 363, 365, 373, 386 and 391. Students should record their evaluation on a record sheet and obtain a witness signature.
- Part two of the assessment might be completed by students on an individual basis or as part of an organised group visit to two travel and/or tourism providers. Although case studies are a useful way of preparing students for this assessment, they will need real contact with an organisation to enable them to evaluate the customer service provided.

The importance of customer service

UNIT 5: PHOTOCOPY MASTER 1

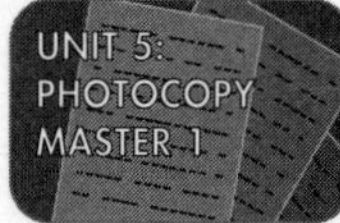

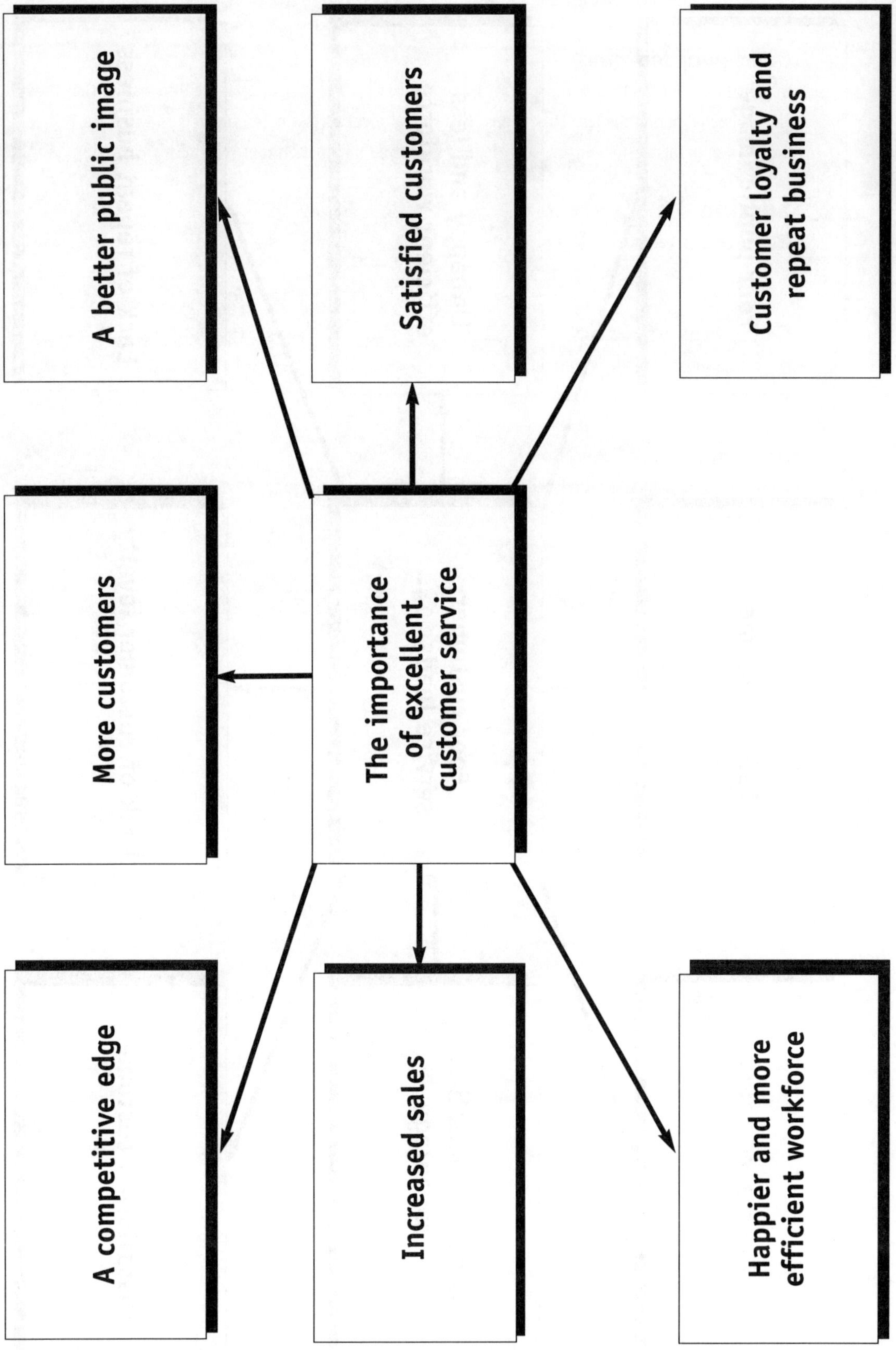

The importance of excellent customer service
A better public image
Satisfied customers
Customer loyalty and repeat business
More customers
A competitive edge
Increased sales
Happier and more efficient workforce

UNIT 5: PHOTOCOPY MASTER 2

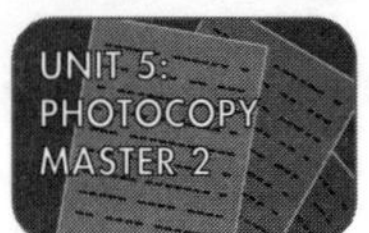

The dangers of poor customer service

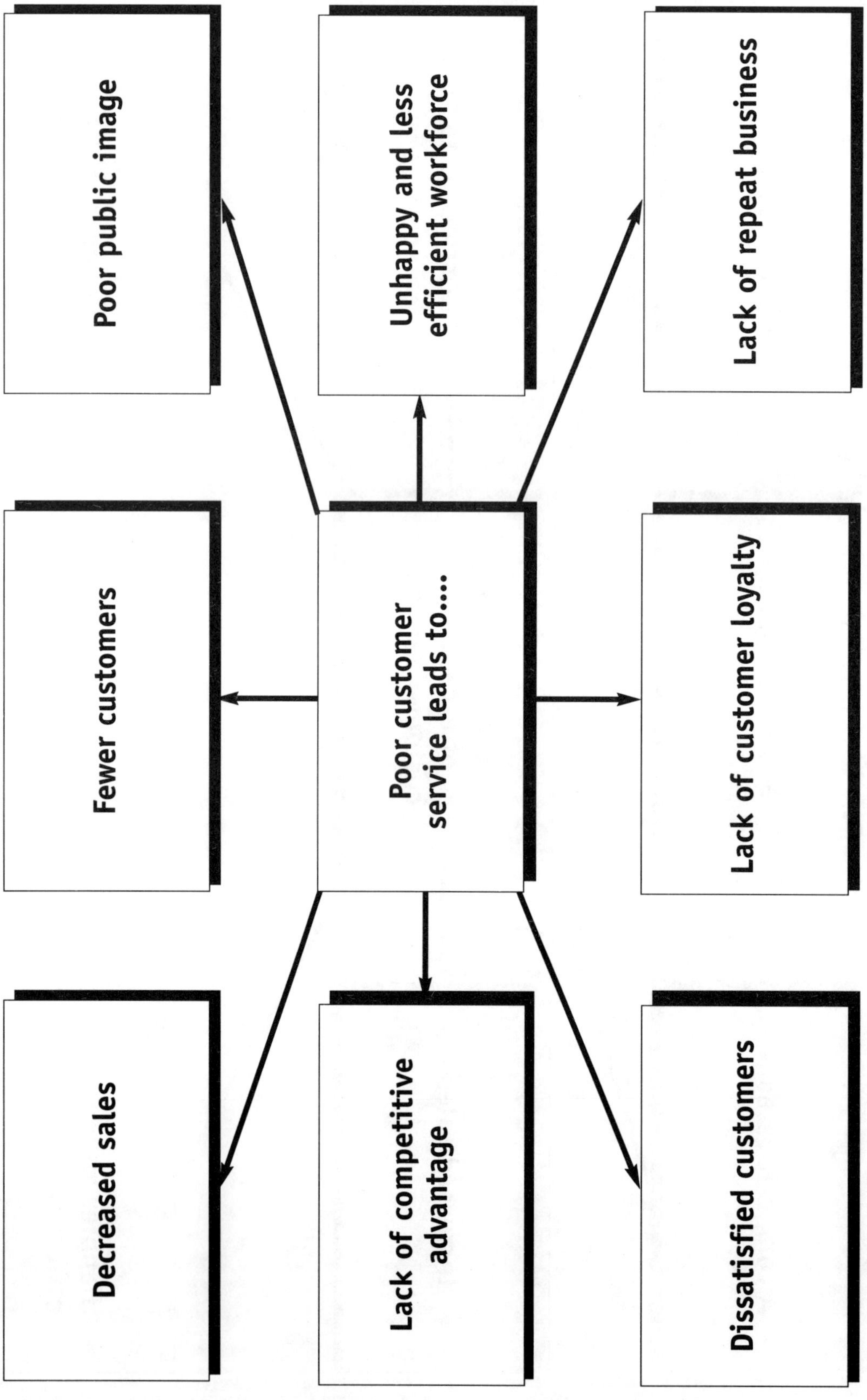

Poor customer service leads to....
Poor public image
Unhappy and less efficient workforce
Lack of repeat business
Fewer customers
Lack of customer loyalty
Decreased sales
Lack of competitive advantage
Dissatisfied customers

Types of customers

UNIT 5: PHOTOCOPY MASTER 3

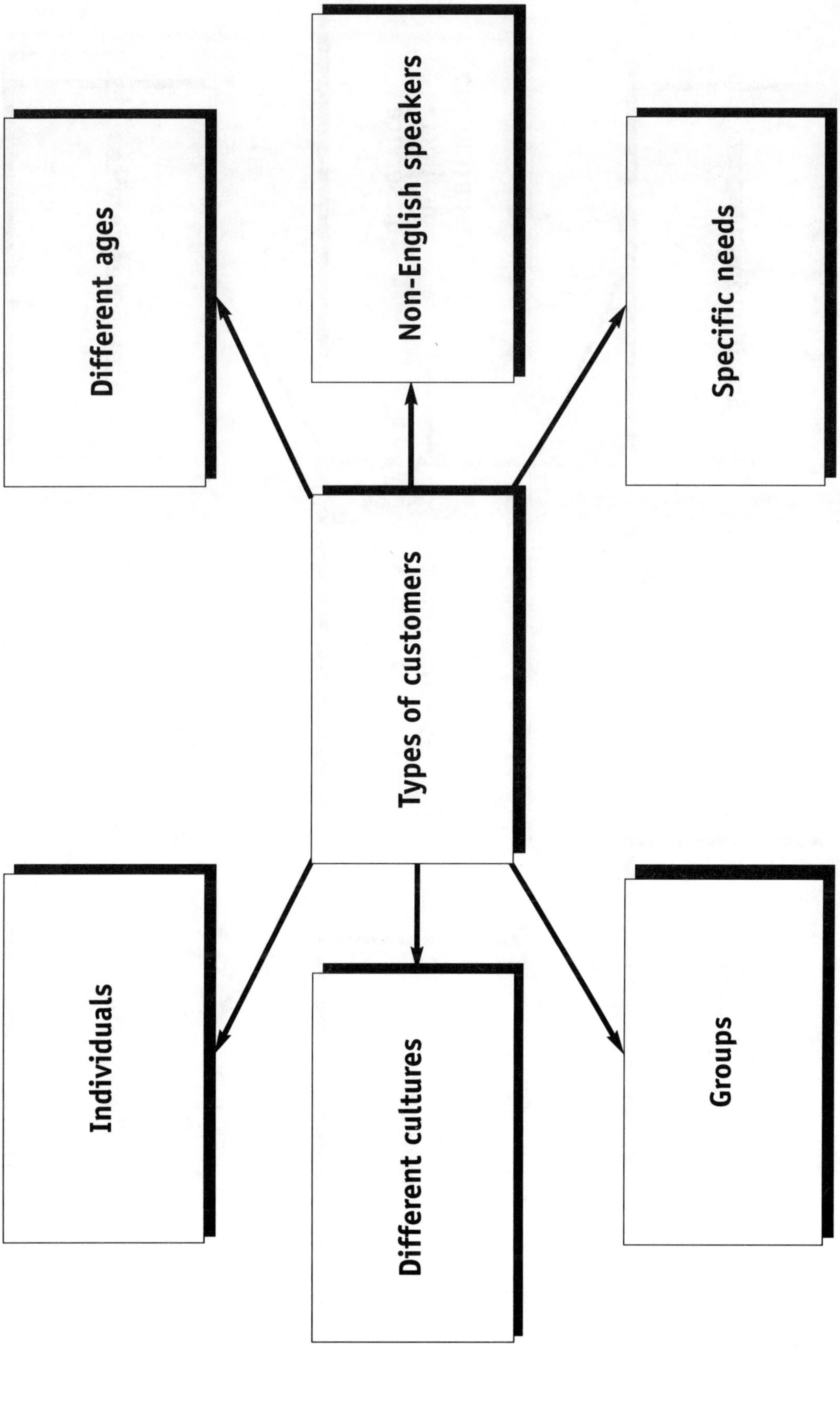

Types of customers

- Different ages
- Non-English speakers
- Specific needs
- Individuals
- Different cultures
- Groups

UNIT 5: PHOTOCOPY MASTER 4

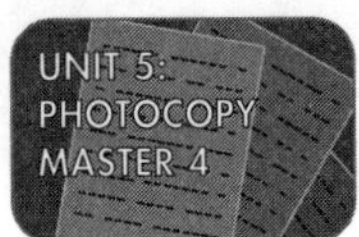

Selling skills

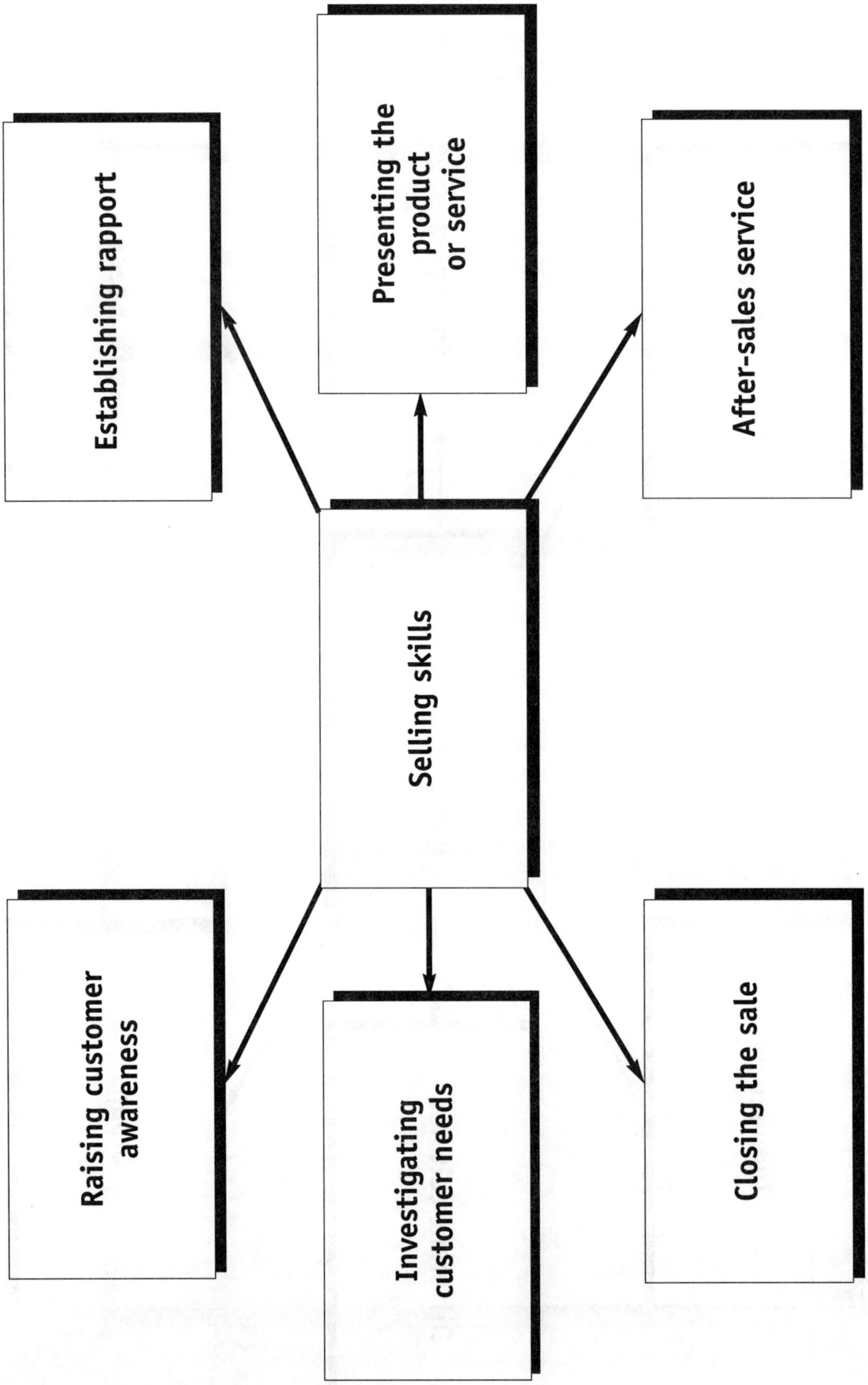

Selling skills
Establishing rapport
Presenting the product or service
After-sales service
Raising customer awareness
Investigating customer needs
Closing the sale

Effective complaint handling

UNIT 5: PHOTOCOPY MASTER 5

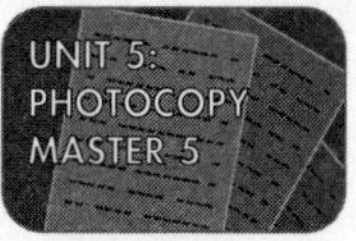

Listen carefully to the customer

↓

Apologise in general terms

↓

Let the customer know that the matter will be investigated

↓

See the problem from the customers point of view

↓

Keep calm and don’t argue

↓

Find a solution or call a supervisor

↓

Agree the solution or call a supervisor

↓

Record details of the complaint/action

UNIT 5: PHOTOCOPY MASTER 6

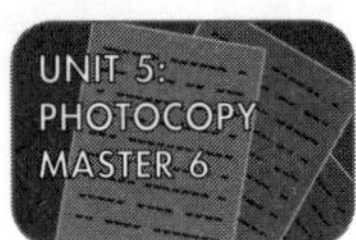

Quality criteria

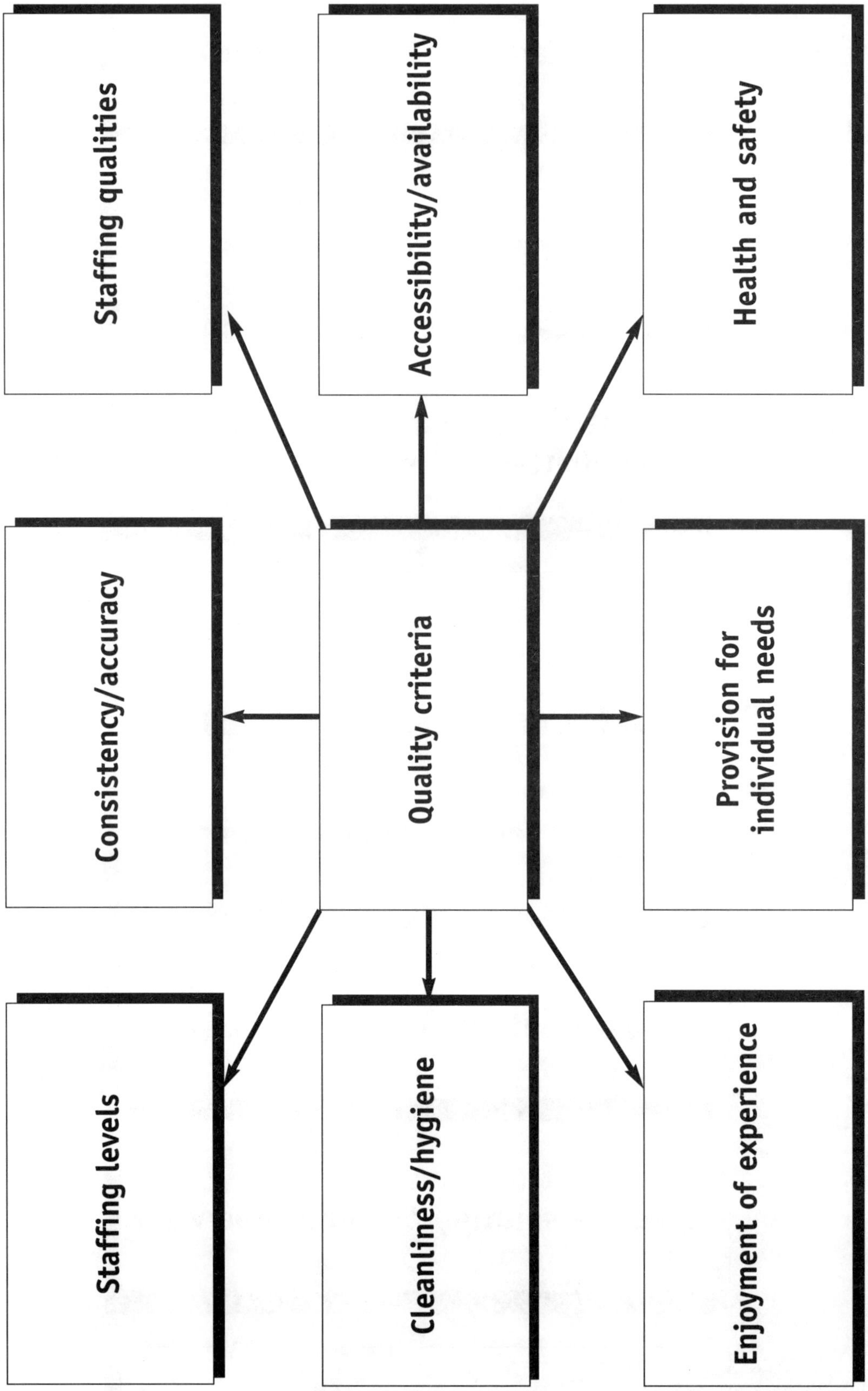

Quality criteria
Staffing qualities
Accessibility/availability
Health and safety
Consistency/accuracy
Provision for individual needs
Staffing levels
Cleanliness/hygiene
Enjoyment of experience

Unit 6:
Travel and tourism in action

Introduction:

This unit brings together the knowledge and skills from other compulsory units – particularly Unit 1 Investigating travel and tourism, Unit 4 Marketing and Unit 5 Customer service – into a practical project. The project can be an event or short business venture, but must be travel and tourism oriented.

Completion of this unit involves students in devising a plan, using teamwork to carry out the project and sharing success as a group, as well as applied travel, tourism and generic business skills. As a result, it is a prime unit for acquiring key skills evidence.

Delivery suggestions

Since this unit requires the use of what has been learnt in other compulsory units, it is best kept until last. However, planning aspects and ideas may need to be started earlier in the year to allow sufficient research and development time.

Unit planner

Session	Session objectives	Text pages
1	To introduce some definitions and examples of projects and events To outline key planning and implementation stages To explain how to record personal involvement in a project	398 to 402
2	To explore ways of generating ideas and options for a suitable project To explain how to assess the feasibility of suitable options	402 to 404
3	To discuss and outline the key elements of a project plan	404 to 407
4	Formulating the key elements of a project plan into a workable business plan for a project: (a) setting aims and objectives	408 to 410
5	Formulating the key elements of a project plan into a workable business for a project: (b) deciding on the timescale and scope of the project	410 to 415
6	Formulating the key elements of a project plan into a workable business plan for a project: (c) identifying customers and devising a marketing strategy	415 to 416
7	Formulating the key elements of a project plan into a workable business plan for a project: (d) using physical and human resources effectively	416 to 421
8	Formulating the key elements of a project plan into a workable business plan for a project: (e) identifying financial resources and budgeting	418 to 420
9	To discuss and consider the allocation of resources identified To identify suitable administration systems to support the project	420 to 422
10	To explore possible legal considerations To explain the process of risk assessment To show how to prepare contingency plans	422 to 429
11	To explain the process of reviewing and evaluating the project To illustrate potential sources of, and methods of gathering, feedback To discuss methods of performance evaluation	430 to 434
12	To discuss and explain how to work as a team To explain the importance of a team structure for the project To identify and discuss roles and responsibilities of team members	435 to 437
13	To explain how to build effective teamwork To identify good leadership skills To show the importance of carrying out a final check	438 to 443
14	To discuss implementing the plan and carrying out the project To discuss evaluation of outcomes of the project	446 to 451
15	To produce assessment evidence for the unit, including: (a) a business plan for the project and (b) a record of involvement in the project	

Session 1

Textbook pages 398 to 402

Resources required

- Case studies of successful travel and tourism projects and events
- OHT 1 on the stages of planning, running and evaluating a project
- Examples of log book pages

Objectives of the session

- To introduce some definitions and examples of projects and events.
- To outline key planning and implementation stages.
- To explain how to record personal involvement in a project.

Development of textbook

- The text tries to set some parameters for projects and events to structure the material in the unit. Use the assessment grid to help students get an understanding of the task ahead of them in this unit.
- Some examples of successful projects and events might prove helpful in the initial stages of discussion. You should draw out the three main stages of projects from these examples: planning, implementation (carrying out plans) and evaluation of outcomes.
- In carrying out a project during the unit, students need to record their inputs and outputs. It is important to embed this discipline of recording project activity at an early stage: the textbook suggests a number of formats, although students could be encouraged to devise their own.
- A distinction needs to be drawn between the 'process' and 'content' of the personal log.

Key words to define

Brainstorming, project, event, feasibility.

Answers to textbook activities

Page 398: Examples of international and national projects and events include the New Orleans Jazz Festival, the carnival in Rio de Janeiro and the Travel Show at Earl's Court (which people travel to from all over the world). Regional events include the Farnborough air show, the Balmoral Highland games, the Eisteddfod in Wales and the Manchester Holiday show. Examples of local projects include stately homes open days, a county show, a motor show and a battle re-enactment.

Page 402:

Process elements:

- schedule for the project – calendar or chart see page 412
- reports on progress – minutes of meetings
- revisions or alterations made – contingency plans or action taken on the spot
- summary of the business plan – an executive one-page summary.

Content elements:

- own contribution – this could be a range of things including ideas, points at a meeting, responsibilities, leadership skills exhibited
- team contribution – such as spirit, cooperation, accomplishments, publicity achieved, funds raised
- adherence to role and briefing – how well this was done, even exceeded, perhaps shown by feedback
- maintenance of health, safety and security – action taken, hazards identified, measures put in place, incidents prevented or handled
- cooperation with others – this really means outside the group, such as with suppliers, officials from other organisations, customers or the press
- how closely the plan was followed – this will allow recording of things that went well as well as those that did not go to plan

- dealing with disruptions – these may have been foreseen or unforeseen, minor or more serious, with repercussions or few consequences, requiring assistance or even causing the project to fail
- advice and guidance sought – this may include tutors and support staff as well as external sources of advice such as such as the police or local authority staff.

Build your learning

Prior to the next session students could be encouraged to bring some suggestions for a project and to begin to draw up their log books.

Session 2

Textbook pages 402 to 404

Resources required

- Flip chart to record ideas

Objectives of the session

- To explore ways of generating ideas and options for a suitable project.
- To explain how to assess the feasibility of suitable options.

Development of the textbook

- A good beginning for this section is a brainstorming session to pick up on students' ideas. Projects should seek to take advantage of local opportunities. A vote could be taken to produce a short list of three projects.
- To avoid spending a great deal of time on unrealistic ideas and proposals, set a time limit for the discussion and appoint a firm student chairperson to direct proceedings.
- A feasibility study will need to be undertaken for each project on the short list. The textbook gives some points which have to be considered, however the feasibility studies may have to consider other factors depending on the scale and ambitions of the three options.
- Roles need to be allocated for the feasibility studies, perhaps with three investigation groups set up, each with a coordinator. This will help show capabilities and raise awareness of team work.
- Before the end of the session, check that each student has made preparations for keeping a log book. Once the project has been selected, it may be easier to decide on the appropriate content and format for the log book.
- A formal session should be organised to review the outcomes of the feasibility studies. Try to compare like with like when assessing the research against the criteria set for the feasibility studies. Choose the final project, following presentations on each option or a minuted discussion.

Key words to define

Ideas and options, feasibility study, personal log book.

Answers to textbook activities

Page 403: Students will have to be realistic in their choices of short-listed projects. Some guidance may have to be given on practical issues which may be unfamiliar to students, such as legal aspects or what is acceptable from the school or college's point of view.

Page 404: The best six are likely to be a distillation of clear aims and objectives, a market for the project, carefully identified resources, legal and safety issues, a detailed plan and set evaluation criteria.

Build your learning

Encourage students to talk to practitioners to gain an insight into the logistics and problems of running a project. In addition, remind them of the need to consider how they will evaluate their efforts and to make entries in their personal logs of their contribution after each meeting or team decision.

Session 3

Textbook pages 404 to 407

Resources required

- OHT 2, the planning and delivery flow chart

Objectives of the session

- To discuss and outline the key elements of a project plan.

Development of the textbook

- The importance of planning cannot be emphasised enough especially if the group has not tackled any similar project before. It is worth running through all aspects of planning – from start to finish – to help students' understanding. The elements of the business plan can be reviewed using the flow chart in OHT 2.
- Explain how the elements of a project plan can be organised into a sequence which can be used to structure a business plan. Leaflets on business plans, produced by most of the major banks, are a useful teaching tool. Some have a do-it-yourself approach that could be used to allow students to work out a suitable format for themselves. It may even be possible to have a businessman's or businesswoman's input to present the practitioner's point of view.

Key words to define

Planning and delivery, process, project management.

Build your learning

This session should be used to set the scene for the more detailed planning that follows in the next sessions. If a clear understanding of the key elements of a project plan can be gained, it will prove valuable later when students need to produce a written version. At this stage, it is worth revisiting the assessment grid to show the importance of each element for the final report.

Session 4

Textbook pages 408 to 410

Resources required

- OHT 2, the planning and delivery flow chart

Objectives of the session

- Formulating the key elements of a project plan into a workable business plan for a project:
  (a) setting aims and objectives.

Development of the textbook

- A clear distinction needs to be made between an aim and an objective: an aim is the overarching vision for the project; an objective is a quantifiable target.
- Allow plenty of time to set project objectives as these will be crucial to progress, achievement and evaluation. The textbook provides examples of different types of objectives which students could customise to their project. Figure 6.7 illustrates the importance of objective setting.
- Use the SMART acronym to keep the purpose of objective setting in students' minds. Once students have agreed aims and objectives, these should be recorded in the business plan. Some means of collating the elements of the business plan – a ring binder, file or computer disk – needs to be agreed as part of the administration of the project.

Key words to define

Aims, objectives, SMART.

Answers to textbook activities

Page 408: This activity should not take too long: the key words need to be short, snappy and memorable. Limit students to one line in their final version.

Page 410: Examples of suitable objectives, with suggestions on evaluation, could include:

- a day trip to a theme park – (objective) to ensure everyone has a park map and an itinerary for the day; (evaluation) check each person individually on the coach on the way to the park and carry spare maps, and by a survey to assess the usefulness of the maps and itinerary
- an outing to a museum – (objective) to ensure there are rest stops and seating during the tour around the museum; (evaluation) site visit to check on loos, seats and a customer survey on the way home
- holding an exhibition – (objective) to fill every stand with an exhibitor and to invite 100 guests; (evaluation) final check a week before the exhibition and visual check on each stand during the exhibition, printing of 120 invites to allow for guests cancelling, and counting the invitations as they are handed in at the entrance
- creating a guide book – (objective) to have a draft copy ready a month before publication and to have 2,000 copies ready for the launch, (evaluation) check progress of material one week before draft stage, and then at the draft ready day, circulate 2,000 copies at the launch
- hosting a quiz – (objective) to have six teams compete in a travel and tourism quiz and to raise £100 for charity; (evaluation) check how many teams appeared and played, and count the amount earned for charity.

Build your learning

One way of helping students with this session is to suggest that they collect mission statements from travel and tourism organisations and event management companies. By analysing these statements, they should find some key words or themes that they can adapt. Students could also study company reports to see the type of aims and objectives that are actually adopted by the industry.

Session 5

Textbook pages 410 to 415

Resources required

- OHT 2, the planning and delivery flow chart
- A calendar or diary for the project
- Blank calendars or flow charts

Objectives of the session

- Formulating the key elements of a project plan into a workable business plan for a project: (b) deciding on the timescale and scope of the project.

Development of the textbook

- The team need to decide on the scope of the project. This needs extensive discussion, covering factors such as the target market, what will be included, when it will run, where it will be held and how it will be staffed. Once these and any other crucial aspects are decided, a draft project description can be written giving the working parameters.
- The timing for a project is a crucial piece of planning, tying the disparate elements together and creating a schedule of tasks. It also creates a sequence against which objectives can be checked regularly. Considerable time should be spent mapping out the timings. The timescale must be adhered to by the project team. Get the team to create deadlines to ensure that key activities are carried out in time.
- Students may present and record their schedule using a range of styles. Their choice may depend on the complexity of the project. The more complex may make use of critical path analysis to help with the scheduling. Some examples of scheduling tools are shown in the textbook.

- By setting priorities, the structure of planning and implementing the project will fall into place. Once created, the schedule should be a standing item on the agenda for team meetings and recorded in the business plan.

Key words to define

Scope, timescale, deadlines, critical path analysis.

Answer to textbook activities

Page 413: Correct order of tasks:

- set regular staff planning meetings
- compile budgets
- agree promotional activities
- design and order posters
- prepare exhibits
- prepare and send out press releases
- prepare and send out invitations
- set up health, safety and security measures
- make hospitality arrangements
- carry out a practice run.

The bar charts should show approximate planning duration times for the three-month project. These are the suggested entries for the 10 tasks:

- staff planning meetings – weekly over three months, for at least an hour
- budgets – two separate meetings in the first week, the first to assess costs, the second to agree budgets
- promotion – a range of activities to cover the target market from one month into the project, including advertisements, press releases, public relations exercises, personal selling activities, a project brochure release
- poster design – daily for the first week, then once again after the poster has been drafted in week three, one final meeting in week four to approve design and check print, a small team can work on this aspect of the project
- exhibits – regularly over three months, this is an ongoing task to be carried out over the project and in the run up to the event
- press releases – monthly releases to keep the project high profile for its duration and one final one during the evaluation phase
- invitations – use the first month to design the invitations and get some verbal assurances from likely guests, then post them out two months ahead of the event day
- health and safety – once final plans are agreed, with two months to go hold a health, safety and security audit (risk assessment); the week after, hold a meeting to agree measures and put them into place at least two weeks before the event
- hospitality – at three months out make provisional booking with a caterer, meet to agree the menu, price and logistics (how and where the food will be served) one month out
- practice run – with a week to go, carry out a practice run.

The critical path analysis would show a single staff meeting, and a similar preparation of exhibits line over the three months supported by tasks 2 to 4 and 6 to 10 feeding into the sequence at the designated times listed above. Key tasks would be the poster design and press releases; these could not go out until all the arrangements were confirmed for the actual exhibition.

For the second part of the activity, use the event planner (Figure 6.10). There is no 'ideal' answer as all projects will be different. However, try to ensure that students adopt good practice wherever possible. Speaking to practitioners is a good basis for comparison of plans.

Build your learning

This crucial session places time-bound parameters on the project which should help student activities. It is worth emphasising that there will always be slippage and some time should be built into the plan to cover unforeseen contingencies – this is sometimes known as 'buffer time'. Transfer timescale parameters into the business plan file and remind students to check progress at regular team meetings.

Session 6

Textbook pages 415 to 416

Resources required

- Printers price list
- Advertising rate card from the local newspaper
- Copies of 'starting a business' leaflet from banks

Objectives of the session

- Formulating the key elements of a project plan into a workable business plan for a project:
  (c) identifying customers and devising a marketing strategy.

Development of the textbook

- Students need to understand the idea of market segmentation, and then carry out some research (during the feasibility stage) to identify the customers that are most likely to be interested in their project or event. The textbook indicates some methods of segmenting likely customers, but students could readily invent their own methods to suit their aims and objectives.
- There is much useful material in Unit 4, Marketing, and Unit 5, Customer Service, that students can draw on. The case study on page 415 also gives a clear indication of how projects can be improved by a customer-oriented approach.
- A diverse range of promotional techniques are illustrated on page 416 of the textbook. Students should choose the techniques that they think will be most effective and appropriate. It is worth reminding students of the need to budget carefully for the costs of advertising and promoting their project.

A good deal of further guidance can be gleaned from bank brochures on starting a business.

Key words to define

Market segmentation, customer service, promotional techniques.

Answers to textbook activities

Page 416: Factors likely to be important in identifying potential customers could be age, lifestyle, income and location. Research techniques include surveys, interviews, observations and focus groups.

A breakeven strategy or objective will probably suggest a low-cost project; a project with an ambitious financial target will probably aim to make a modest profit. Students will also have to assess if the project is price sensitive – is price an important factor for potential customers?

Figure 6.13 gives the standard range of promotional techniques, students may have a more innovative approach.

Students may need to contact printers, newspapers, outside venues and the post office for prices – or have an equivalent cost attached to any work which is done for free in school or college – in order to get accurate costs for their business plan.

Build your learning

It is worth reminding students that the next stage of planning concerns more tangible and practical aspects of the project that depend on resources. It would be useful to ask students to think through what might be required to implement the project – both in terms of physical and human resources – and bring a list for the next session.

Session 7

Textbook pages 416 to 421

Resources required

- Access to any venue used for the project or event

Objectives of the session

- Formulating the key elements of a project plan into a workable business plan for a project: (d) using physical and human resources effectively.

Development of the textbook

- This section moves a little away from the traditional planning sequence in considering physical and human resources together, but it helps by getting students to consider these aspects before the next session, which is devoted to financial planning and budgeting.
- There is unlikely to be a definitive list of physical resources and students may need some help over the more technical or legal requirements. The textbook mentions a range of physical resources to give an indication of what might need to be included. It also suggests some ways in which groups can create lists of likely resource needs.
- When compiling resources needs, suggest that students adopt the KISS principle: keep it short and simple. Encourage students to draw up a realistic list, which is attainable and affordable. Students should be advised to use school or college resources to help reduce costs. Hiring venues and equipment can cause problems for this age group. There can be contractual problems, especially if the institution's name is to be associated with the arrangements.
- Human resources will, of course, start with the students themselves, but could be extended to involve family, friends, staff and outside organisations, all of which will need managing. Getting the right people for the right tasks is not easy, so teams need to plan this aspect of the project carefully. Also, post project, remind students to thank those who gave their time freely during the project.
- Once the tasks which individuals will carry out have been described and allocated, it is worth keeping a written record in case of personnel and role changes. Each team member should have specific roles to play, so team meetings should have a session about roles to help clarify who is doing what.
- Session 12 on teamwork covers other relevant human resource topics in more depth.

Key words to define

Physical resources, human resources, KISS principle, roles.

Answers to textbook activities

Page 417: Here is a possible answer, although many other resources could be added and it is not meant to be a fully comprehensive list:

- ensure five teams attend – invitations, flyers, reply-paid envelopes, entry forms, signs
- ensure five teams obtain sponsorship – guidance notes on obtaining sponsors, team member sponsorship sheets
- create the obstacle course – gymnastic equipment such as trampette, vaulting box, nets, ropes, benches, tyres, crash mats, and so on
- provide catering – small kitchen, drinks, snacks, fruit, washing up facilities
- handle finances – petty cash float, secure box, record book, receipts
- obtain prizes – letter of support, donations
- ensure safety – risk assessment of venue and equipment, first aider on hand, mobile phone
- thank teams, sponsors and venue – circular letter, envelopes, stamps.

This activity has potential for expansion by identifying resources we have missed or not listed. Refer students to the Alton Towers' example in Figure 6.14 to reinforce the approach.

Page 418: The actual resources will, of course, vary from project to project, however the process of checking their readiness for use usually comes closer to the actual date of the project start. In general terms, actions which need to be taken to ensure readiness include that resources:

- are still available on the day
- have been properly maintained
- are suitable for the purpose, for example strong enough
- are there in sufficient quantity
- are durable
- are insured (if required)
- are affordable
- will be delivered and returned on time
- can be used correctly by team members.

Page 421: These suggestions are by no means comprehensive but do give generic tasks that are likely to be appropriate to most projects.

- **Finance:** costing resources, projecting income and expenditure, collecting fees, accounting for ticket sales, recording sponsorship monies, preparing profit or loss totals, balancing books at the end of the project, paying bills, giving receipts, checking budgets.
- **Human resources:** finding team members to carry out tasks, checking people have done their jobs, motivating team members, supporting people in carrying out their responsibilities, enforcing any rules and procedures required to be followed by people, finding volunteers communicating with people involved, meeting customers.
- **Marketing:** carrying out research, identifying customers, preparing promotional activities, designing publicity material, looking after client needs or quality issues.
- **Security:** checking the venue for hazards, providing a cloakroom service, dealing with contingencies, observing proceedings, preventing the opportunity for petty theft, directing people or cars.
- **Physical resources:** room allocation, equipment needs, providing materials, liaison with suppliers, checking access for disabled customers, communication systems.

Build your learning

Undoubtedly a site visit helps with the resources assessment, as will training or practice sessions to use equipment with which the team is not familiar. The dress rehearsal, or dry run, should show up any omissions or inadequacies in resources, or peoples' inability to use them or fulfil their role in the project. Ensure that all resource lists are included in the official business plan records and that anyone responsible for resources has a copy. Make this a standing item at meetings.

Session 8

Textbook pages 418 to 420

Resources required

- Accounting paper for creation of budgets
- Access to sources of information on costs
- Spreadsheet programs
- Check lists of other resources and the promotional activities

Objectives of the session

- Formulating the key elements of a project plan into a workable business plan for a project:
  (e) identifying financial resources and budgeting.

Development of the textbook

- Start with a clear definition of what is meant by managing financial resources. It covers accounting for all income and expenditure, preparing and sticking to a budget, and monitoring and controlling cash flow
- As most projects will only have a small financial content, a simple record could be made in a cash book. Before briefing students, check whether they must adhere to any school or college procedures for handling money.
- As there is likely to be a financial objective in the project, explain the breakeven principle and how to set a profit margin. A sound grasp of the concept of budgeting and cash flow are also needed.
- If the team is successful in attracting a sponsor, consider appointing one member of the team to look after the sponsorship deal. Dealing with money is not the only competence tested in a sponsorship relationship.
- Stress that proper records should be kept, either on a paper format or on a spreadsheet. The use of the KISS principle applies here – keep it short and simple! All cash-flow forecasts need to be recorded in the business plan for the duration of the project. As with other aspects of planning financial reporting should take place at every team meeting.
- At completion, the financial records need to 'balance' to show what cash or assets have been used or are left. These records will be used to evaluate the financial performance of the project.

Key words to define

Income, expenditure budget, cash flow, financial objectives, records (accounts), sponsorship, KISS principle, financial performance.

Answers to textbook activities

Page 419: Many of our suggestions could be applied to all scenarios, so view the whole list as possible solutions.

- **Scenario one** – the group could contact the suppliers to see if they have a record of amounts; approval for spending could be made subject to two signatures; if the team finds that the overspend is necessary, the marketing budget should be increased to cover the additional costs; if the team finds the overspend unacceptable, the person responsible might be made to repay some of the money; £40 will have to be found from another source to cover the overspend.
- **Scenario two** – stronger financial control should have been exercised; an audit of how money was spent needs to be carried out; proposals of how to repay the outstanding debt need to made; further fund-raising may have to be undertaken to pay off the debt.
- **Scenario three** – first of all the group need to check what price applied when it made the booking (perhaps it was the old lower price); the organisation hiring out the venue may, as a gesture to the students, forego the increased price; good contingency planning may mean that some money has been held in reserve; a sponsor could be perhaps be found at short notice to cover this cost; the group might make a special appeal for help, perhaps on the radio or to the school or college principal.
- **Scenario four** – a special meeting could be called for to make all participants account for the money they raised and to make contingency to chase up sponsors; a letter could be sent to all sponsors explaining the situation and asking them to pay; this would have to be authenticated by someone in authority, contain an apology for the problem, plus some evidence that the participant had actually completed the walk; the cost of the trip could be trimmed.

Session 9

Textbook pages 420 to 422

Resources required

- OHT 2, business plan flow chart
- Computer system to create records

Objectives of the session

- To discuss and consider the allocation of resources identified.
- To identify suitable administration systems to support the project.

Development of the textbook

- Most student projects will run to a tight budget so the importance of allocating resources effectively and efficiently is paramount. Students should be encouraged to plan this carefully not to assume 'it will be alright on the night'.
- Guidance is given in the text, however as projects will vary greatly the following simple principles might be useful: don't duplicate spending or use of resources; get things for free if possible; be fair in resource allocation. If a particular resource is not affordable or available, consider altering the plans to do without that aspect of the project or find a substitute. Set some criteria for the use of resources, such as cost effectiveness, flexibility, availability, usefulness for the whole team.
- Allocation and use of resources is often linked to the administration system that a team sets up to deal with its project needs. An effective system should support the use of resources and good communication. Here again the KISS principle can be a useful reminder for students: keep it short and simple. Regular checks at meetings should ensure systems are functioning for the team's benefit, if not adjustments can be agreed.
- Systems adapted for project use are likely to be for taking bookings, producing publicity materials or tickets, recording data, communicating with staff, customers and other team members, recording personal involvement and evaluation records. Use of a computer software package is likely to be a must.

Key words to define

Resource allocation, administration systems.

Answers to textbook activities

Page 422: The programme needs to be split into activities and time blocks then resources allocated to each such as:

- greeting at the school or college – a two-person team (human resources) of good confident communicators, with prospectuses and mementos (physical resources)
- a guided tour – to be done in small groups with five tour guides (human resources)
- tour activities – using computers (physical resources), introduction to the principal (human resources)
- lunch – to be bought for them (financial resources)
- travel to the attraction – coach to venue (physical resources), no fee (financial resources)
- entry and tour – entry fee paid (financial resources), guides (human resources)
- return to their accommodation – coach provided (physical resources)
- evening – meal for everyone (guests to pay), then taken to a club by host students (human resources).

Build your learning

Careful agreement has to be reached on the allocation and use of resources according to budget and activity requirements. Anything agreed needs to be recorded for future consultation and evaluation. Students could split resource use into 'routine' and 'non-routine' or allocate resources on a functional basis for the business plan. If a computer system is used, ensure everyone knows how to use it and that there is backup.

Session 10

Textbook pages 422 to 430

Resources required

- OHT 3, major legislation
- Samples of health, safety and security policies
- Information on the HSE and EU regulations
- Samples of insurance policy documents

Objectives of the session

- To explore possible legal considerations.
- To explain the process of risk assessment.
- To show how to prepare contingency plans.

Development of the textbook

- Students may at first be wary of handling the legal issues due to lack of knowledge, and you should make it clear that they need only know the key aims and applications of the legislation not the exact detail. Projects will be very diverse and may need to take account of a wide range of legislation, so a good awareness needs to be created. Figure 6.18, summary of the main regulations, could be a useful starting point.
- Introduce the Health and Safety Executive and use it as the main source of information and guidance throughout. Figure 6.17 in the textbook, on page 423, summarises some of the benefits of having a good health and safety policy, and could be used as the basis for a discussion.
- The concept of risk assessment– the basis for legislation today – needs to be thoroughly understood by students. The concepts of probability and severity as they relate to risk assessment can be usefully covered here. Insurance and liability also come into this section, together with security issues.
- The session might conclude with a look at contingency planning, in effect the measures put in place to deal with hazards, unforeseen circumstances and accidents should they happen. Students need to hold a specific meeting to explore the issues brought up by health, safety, security and dealing with contingencies. The measures agreed need to be put into the business plan and copies circulated to everyone in the team for reference (and for inclusion in their personal log).

Key words to define

Contingency planning, Health and Safety Executive, hazards, risk assessment, legal considerations, insurance and liability.

Answers to textbook activities

Page 427 'Legal considerations': The answers are Data Protection Act, Health and Safety at Work Act, Children Act, Fire Precautions Act and Food Safety Act

Page 427 'Insurance': Projects might require a range of insurance to cover travel, loss or theft of goods, medical, cancellation, public liability, accidents and damage. Students should find that much will be covered by their institution's policy, but these factors do need checking before a project goes ahead, especially if the public are involved.

Page 428 'Security risk assessment':

- A three-day arts event – theft of pictures or exhibits, damage to paintings, people sneaking in for free.
- A gathering of vintage cars – vandalisation of the cars, theft of cars or parts, damage to bodywork.
- Trip to Paris – students getting lost or left behind, accidents, theft or loss of possessions, loss of passports or tickets, short changing of currency.

Page 428: 'Legal risk assessment': Remind students to cover the five steps to risk assessment (set out on page 425) in health, safety, security and insurance, respectively. Refer to work done with contingency planning.

Page 430:

- The missing child – Check at the entrance in case she has been found, if not report her missing and give details. Have staff walk around the main paths calling and looking for her. Ask the staff of the facility to initiate their contingency plans for a lost child. Call the police. Ensure the rest of the group are safe and not troubled by her disappearance. Check her personal details for any medical or other conditions. Inform the emergency contact person and her parents if necessary.

- Coach breaks down – Have the driver radio or signal for help. Start some guessing games or a sing song if the party in the bus are becoming difficult. Check if someone has a mobile phone to call for assistance.
- Wedding carriage doesn't appear – Call the company to see what has happened. Have someone call a taxi. Use a friend's car. Check how long it would take for a hire car to arrive. Check if the couple have a travel deadline and ring ahead to say there will be a delay.
- Generator packs up – Check whether the generator has run out of fuel. Call an engineer. Try to hire another one. Move to other premises. Reschedule the event. Find an alternative source of heating.
- Torrential rain – Encourage people to take taxis instead and come back when the field has dried out. Try to use four-wheel drive vehicles to help tow people out. Put down ramps or gravel to help traction. Set up a team of 'pushers'. Have people call the RAC or AA for assistance. Call the police to redirect traffic.
- Caterer fails to turn up – Call another one quickly. Pick up the food in cars. Go out and buy some ready-made sandwiches. Find a team of sandwich makers and do it yourself.
- Coach fails to turn up – Call the coach company or driver if you have their numbers. Call home to say there is a delay. Try to find a replacement. Find something interesting for the group to do while the whole affair is sorted out.
- Team member falls ill – Have the leader step in until a replacement can be found. Give the missing person's role to someone else in the team. Call the person to see if they can help over the phone or can brief a replacement. Reschedule their input. Modify the project.

Build your learning

An extension of the activity on legal considerations (page 427) could prove a useful aid for helping students to understand where and how legislation and regulations are applied. Some further case studies or scenarios could be created to complement those given and might be contextualised to projects.

Session 11

Textbook pages 430 to 434

Resources required

- Examples of performance evaluation and criteria from the industry
- Sample questionnaires
- Spreadsheets of data, graphics of data

Objectives of the session

- To explain the process of reviewing and evaluating the project.
- To illustrate potential sources of, and methods of gathering, feedback.
- To discuss methods of performance evaluation.

Development of the textbook

- The importance of SMART objective setting needs to be emphasised at the outset. To help with motivation, encourage students to think of collecting their evidence in diverse ways, this will also serve the purpose of cross-referencing data later.
- Explain what feedback is and how it needs to tie into performance evaluation criteria so that questions asked produce material that can actually be used for evaluation. Each area of the business plan may need evaluation criteria.
- The textbook gives guidance on areas which need evaluation, sources of evidence and methods of presenting the data. Performance evaluation should be given in both quantitative and qualitative forms, and this may need explaining at the outset.
- Gathering feedback needs to be well coordinated, for some will be taken part way through the project, not just at the end. Sufficient time, therefore, needs to be allowed in the schedule for this function. The textbook provides suggestions on feedback collection and the type of information required. Methods of gathering feedback should be entered into the business plan.

- Discuss and review feedback in a sensitive and constructive way, so that students are not offended if the report is poor. No team can get everything right: there are sure to be problem areas, and these should be expected even if they can't be anticipated. The evaluation should cover how the team coped under pressure. Students should note the main findings in their personal log books.

Key words to define

Performance criteria, performance evaluation, feedback, data presentation

Build your learning

Graphical presentation of feedback and performance data can be very effective. Students should agree how they will do this, for it might influence the form in which data is collected.

Session 12

Textbook pages 435 to 437

Resources required

- OHT 4, showing a likely team structure for a project
- Sample job descriptions
- Case studies of good teamwork
- Examples of minutes and agendas

Objectives of the session

- To discuss and explain how to work as a team.
- To introduce and explain the importance of a team structure for the project.
- To identify and discuss roles and responsibilities of team members.

Development of the textbook

- The textbook starts by defining a team and giving some examples to help show the need for a structure to cover team and task functions, authority and communications. Emphasise that teams don't just happen; they are created and perpetuated by good leaders and good team members. Use some examples to illustrate the process – perhaps our Olympians, or the England football team (to show the opposite).
- Project teams are usually formed on an ad hoc basis. The merits and workings of a committee structure can be used as a contrast and to prompt discussion about what is better for the project. Roles and responsibilities should be based on written briefs so there is no doubt about what someone is supposed to do. These can be held in personal logs for evaluation purposes later.
- The role of the leader and coordinator is crucial and some discussion over which person (or persons) is best suited for this role should be encouraged. Leaders will need to be competent and confident in dealing with conflict, delegation, decision making, motivation, discipline, and so on.
- Election of a small leadership team may help share the burden and could be adapted to fit the project needs and structure. This will help spread responsibilities and give support to other members of the project team. Deputies can also be elected to cover in the absence of a key person.

Key words to define

Team structure, roles, responsibilities, agendas, minutes.

Answers to textbook activities

Page 437: Job descriptions should cover aspects such as job title, scope of the job, training, tasks to be completed, performance standards, methods to be used.

Build your learning

Students may need some time to find the best structure and to create the job specifications and briefing sheet. Most HRM texts are useful for this purpose. You might provide suitable HR texts on team building.

Session 13

Textbook pages 438 to 443

Resources required

- OHT 5, showing models of teamwork

Objectives of the session

- To explain how to build effective teamwork.
- To identify good leadership skills.
- To show the importance of carrying out a final check.

Development of the textbook

- Tuckman's sequence explains the group dynamics. It provides a useful evaluation structure too. The article on page 439 of the textbook shows how high-performance teams must function to survive and be 'winners'. Some other case studies could be brought in closer to students interests to help make points.
- Dealing with conflict is probably going to be the biggest area of focus for team leaders and members. Some scenarios or role plays could be usefully set to bring these points home. The textbook provides some examples of key factors affecting performance which may come out in the evaluation after the project. Emphasise the value of good communications throughout the project. It is the glue which holds the efforts together.
- Some theoretical underpinning on leadership and team types is included to help give depth of understanding and allow deeper evaluation of the team's performance. Synergy is a key concept, and a useful way of summarising the teambuilding process and potential outcomes. Getting the right atmosphere (team spirit) in the team is absolutely crucial to create the 'feel-good factor'.
- The last pre-implementation act which the team must carry out is a final check. This can come in the form of a dry run, a dress rehearsal or just a meeting to talk it all through and recap. Some form of check list needs to be created so that things which go according to plan can be noted, and anything which does not can be revised as appropriate.

Key words to define

Effectiveness, leadership styles, contingency approach, delegation, closing the loop, conflict, Belbin's team types, leadership theories, synergy, dry run.

Answers to textbook activities

Page 440 'BT Global Challenge': Key issues might include:

- selecting team members – how will this be done?
- inexperience, nervousness, shyness – how will this be overcome?
- attention to detail – some people are better at this
- pressure to deliver – will mount as the project approaches
- stress of responsibility – who will remain cool?
- having a strategy – refer to the plan
- settings targets – appropriate for the team and individuals
- being consistent – in dealing with everyone
- good communications – from start to finish
- creating a 'no blame culture' – a good team environment is needed
- decision making – firm, fair and fast
- supporting each other – even when things go wrong
- standards of behaviour and tolerance – how does the team set standards
- friendship – will it be maintained or lost through conflict.

Page 440 'Group dynamics': It will be luck if the group succeeds in untangling themselves. The underlying aim is to create a dynamic of communication, cooperation and break down physical barriers.

Page 441 'Leadership styles': The insistence on a log book check shows an autocratic style. Allowing the team to vote on the practice is more democratic. Leaving them to do their own recording unchecked is laissez faire.

Page 433: Most effective teams, according to Belbin's research, have a balance of members to help cover the range of skills required to be successful. Too many 'plants', for example, or 'shapers' can set up conflicts. Teams, however, can afford to have a few good 'team workers' as long as there is a good leader. Every team needs a 'completer -finisher' to see to the fine details right to the end. Some analogies can be drawn with sports teams to aid understanding.

Page 444:

- Team: the right atmosphere and good support; motivation and leadership; trust and cooperation; a good plan, but flexibility.
- Task: reward for completion; shared roles; clear descriptions; tangible progress.
- Individual: something in it for them; a sense of belonging; confidence; positive outcomes.

Build your learning

Closing the loop means being able to plan a task, do it, review how it was done, and feed that into how you tackle the next task. Students could be asked to give some examples of when they have done this in real life.

Students need to be primed to record details of how the team actually performed in comparison to the objective set at the outset. Some thought needs to go into how to record this information.

Session 14

Textbook pages 446 to 451

Resources required

- Copies of the business plan
- Personal logs
- Surveys and any other feedback materials

Objectives of the session

- To discuss implementing the plan and carrying out the project.
- To discuss evaluation of outcomes of the project.

Development of the textbook

- Draw the six reminder points for implementing the plan (listed on page 446 of the textbook) to the students' attention. Some examples are included, but the suggestions are by no means exhaustive and could usefully be extended and expanded to suit a particular project's planned needs.
- The case studies show how meticulously well researched and planned a project has to be to guarantee its success. Health, safety and security are often forgotten in the excitement of running the project, so a timely reminder is included at this point.
- As tutors, you may consider that an aspect of the plan has been too loosely organised and an indirect reminder of its importance may prove useful. This is at your discretion, but if the public are involved a small intervention may prevent negative outcomes, such as bad publicity, illegal activities or conflict, or poor learning.
- The evaluation session should be held a short time after the event to allow data to be collected and individual logs to be written up. This means that evidence is to hand for the meeting. At the evaluation meeting there should be the original project objectives, the business plan, any individual targets or deadlines, personal logs, minutes of meetings, feedback gathered, survey results, publicity generated,

video or photographic evidence, comments taken from professionals consulted and incident reports.

- The team should work through the evidence and evaluate where objectives were (a) met, (b) not met and (c) exceeded. It would also be useful to have the assessment grid available for reference.
- The group needs to pool their evidence and draw some conclusions on the planning and carrying out of their project. Where areas are found to be wanting, some recommendations should be made for future reference.

Key words to define

Evaluation, evaluation techniques, keeping to the team plan, evidence, recommendations.

Answers to textbook activities

Page 447: Examples of good practice include:

- the Chichesters avoided borrowing too much which would have increased their 'risk'
- they kept some other options open until the final figures (feasibility study) confirmed their main choice
- they checked with the local authority that what they planned was able to go ahead
- they were careful to respect the environment in the project's development plan, and followed conditions set out for them
- they carried out accurate cash flow projections which impressed and convinced the bank to lend them money
- safety features were installed
- contingency funds were organised to cover unseen factors
- an effective marketing plan was put in place
- an evaluation was carried out at the end of the development stage
- a computer was installed to improve efficiency and capabilities for the future.

Build your learning

Students could use the Young Enterprise skills profile (Figure 6.30) to benchmark and evaluate the project.

Session 15

Textbook pages 451

Resources required

- The assessment grid
- Copies of all feedback materials, the business plan and personal logs
- OHTs 1–5

Objectives of the session

- To produce assessment evidence for the unit, including:
  (a) a business plan for the project
  (b) a record of involvement in the project.

Development of the textbook

- This session should follow on from the evaluation meeting, in which all evidence will have been made available, conclusions drawn and recommendations made.
- Use the OHTs to prompt students. Make sure that they refer to the assessment grid, their logs, their business plan, minutes of team meetings and the evaluation meeting findings.
- Advise that inclusion and correct use of theory in their assessment will indicate a deeper understanding, as will evidence of creativity and innovation.
- Evaluation and evidence showing a high level of responsibility – carried out well – will indicate potential for a higher grade. Similarly, critical analysis and realistic recommendations indicates potential for a high grade.

Planning and implementation loop

UNIT 6:
PHOTOCOPY
MASTER 1

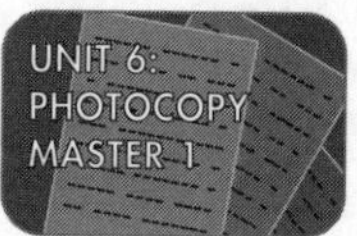

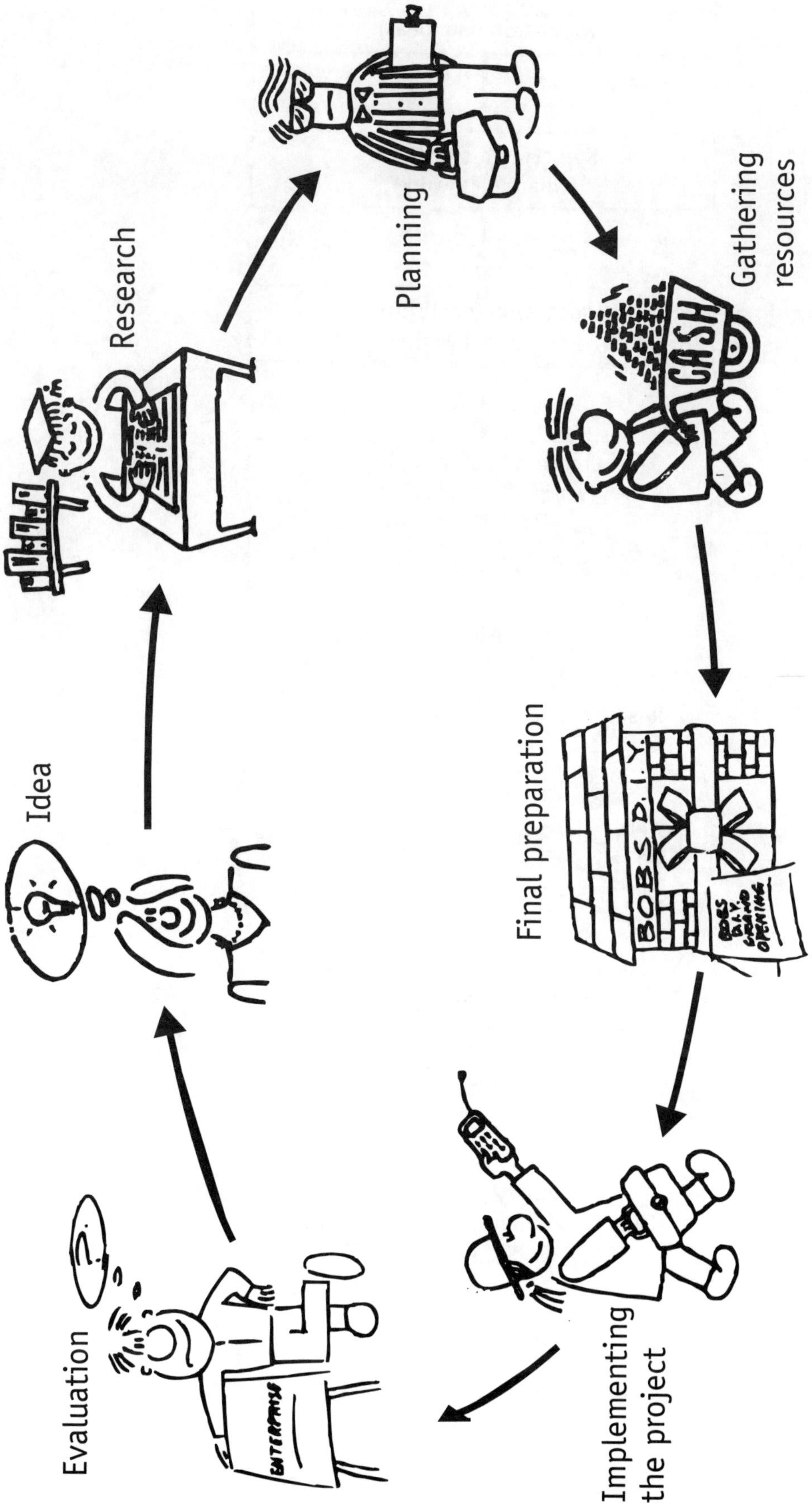

Idea
Research
Planning
Gathering resources
CASH
Final preparation
BOBS D.I.Y.
BOBS D.I.Y. GRAND OPENING
Implementing the project
Evaluation
ENTERPRISE

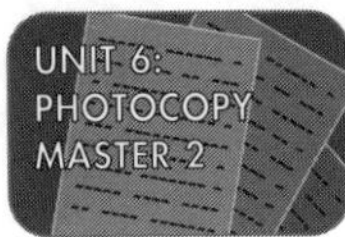

Planning and delivery flow chart

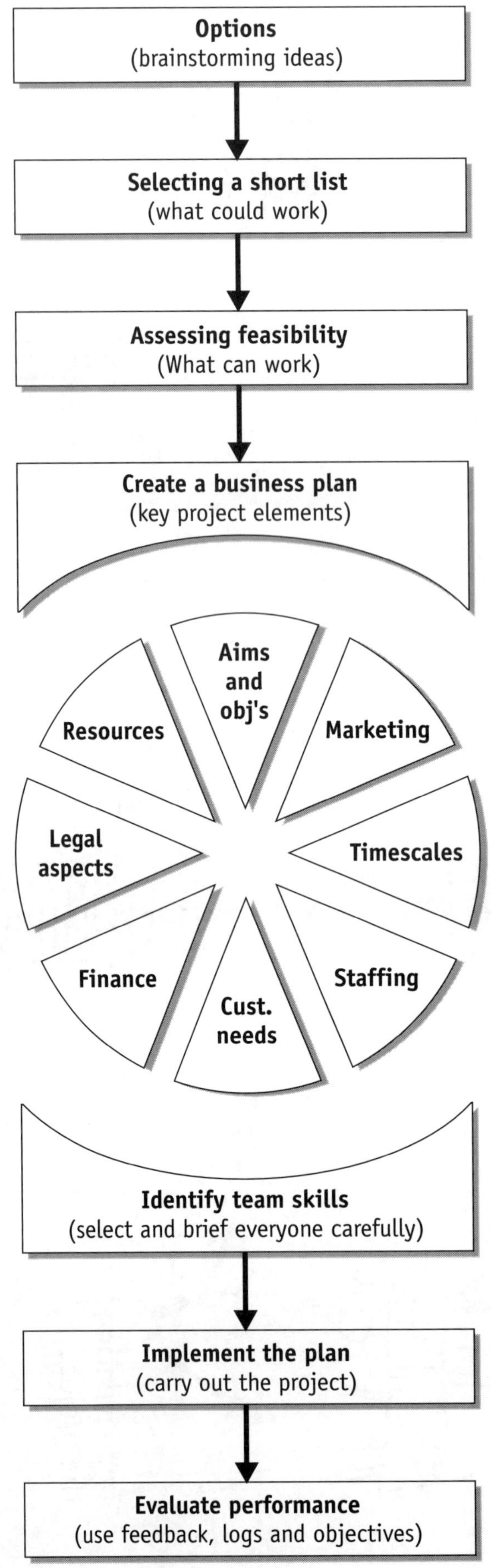

Scheduling bar chart for travel and tourism event

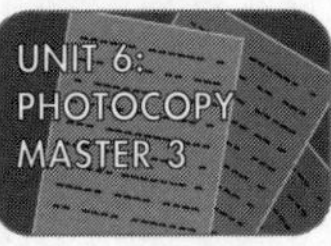

Task	Week ending (Friday) 8 Jan	15 Jan	22 Jan	29 Jan	5 Feb	12 Feb	19 Feb	26 Feb	5 Mar	12 Mar	19 Mar
Agree plan for event	■	■									
Design layout			■	■	■						
Identify and book speakers					■	■					
Prepare publicity					■						
Allocate materials and resources						■	■				
Agree contingencies							■				
Check arrangements								■			
Liaison with exhibitors	■	■			■	■		■	■		
Final press releases									■		
Stage event										■	
Gather and evaluate data										■	■

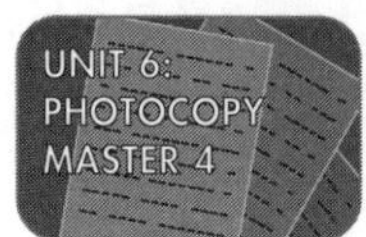

Example of a structure for a project team

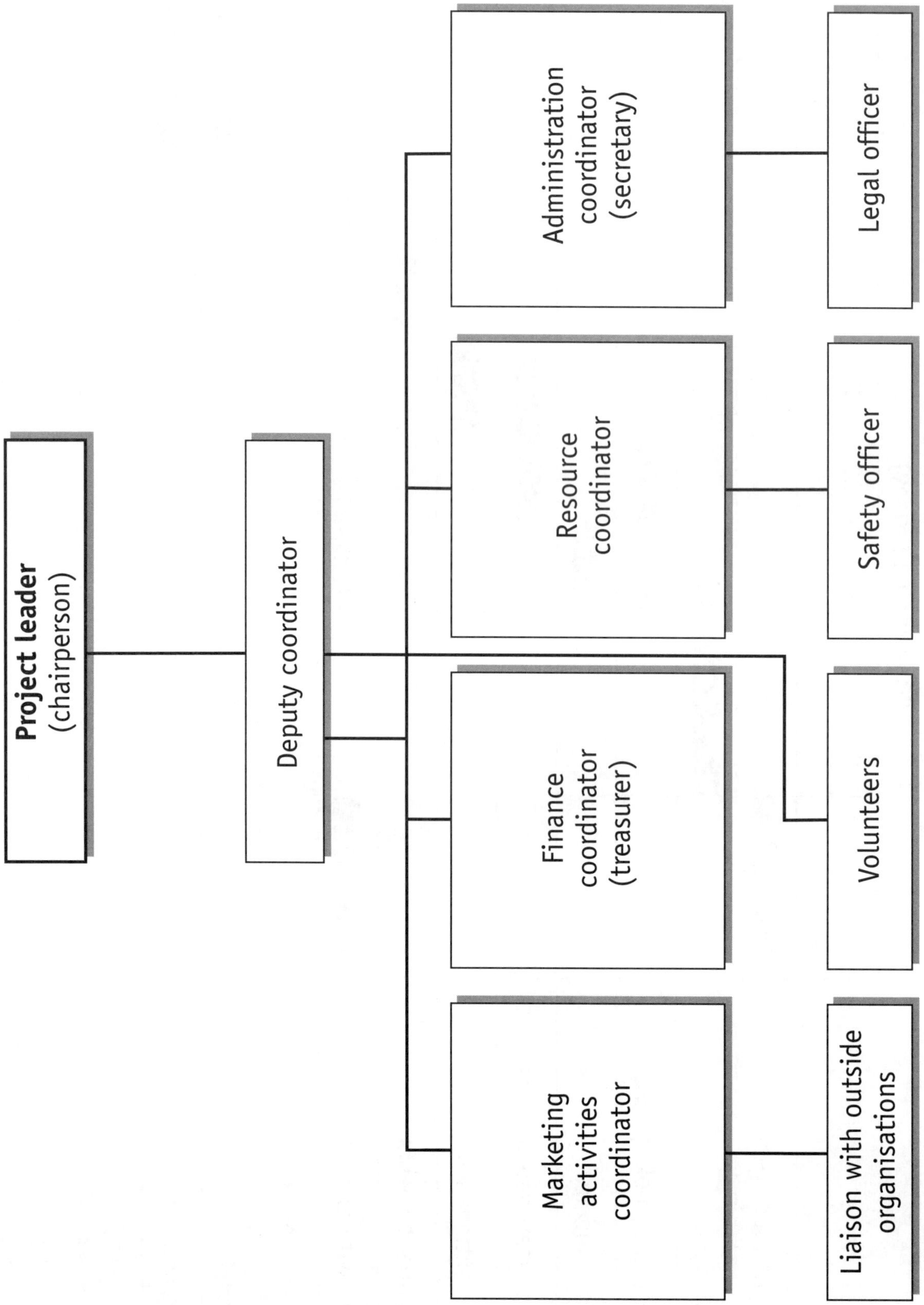

Project leader
(chairperson)

Deputy coordinator

Marketing activities coordinator

Finance coordinator (treasurer)

Resource coordinator

Administration coordinator (secretary)

Liaison with outside organisations

Volunteers

Safety officer

Legal officer

Effective teamwork

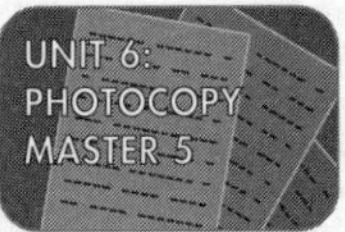

TASK

INDIVIDUAL

TEAM

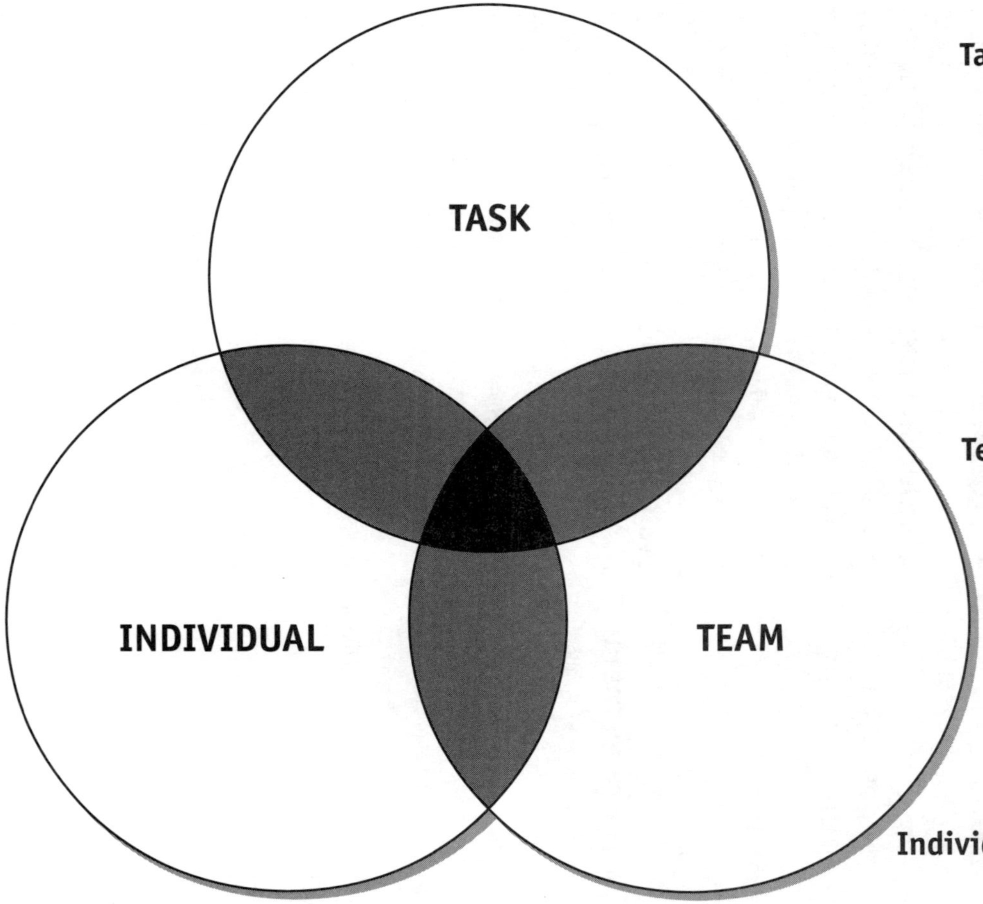

Key

- ■ Leadership at the heart
- ■ Communication linking the areas

Task:

- Clear goals
-
-
-
-

Team:

- Good communication
-
-
-
-

Individual:

- Clear roles
-
-
-
-

Developing work-relatedness

Work placement

Work placement is not a requirement of the Vocational A level in Travel and Tourism. However, there are a wide range of benefits to students in making it a recognised part of the course. These benefits include:

- experiencing a real working environment within the travel and tourism industries
- putting into practice some of the skills and knowledge that have been gained during the course
- developing and improving personal skills, such as working as a member of a team, time management and dealing with customers
- collecting assessment evidence, both for the vocational units and the key skills units
- gaining insight into career opportunities.

Selecting suitable work placements

Tutors may help students arrange work placements or expect students to identify and arrange their own work placements. Whichever of these options is chosen, it is important that students select a placement based on recognised and understood criteria. Students can use a number of criteria when identifying and selecting a suitable work placement. Students might use the planning for work placement pro forma (see page 142 of this pack). They should certainly consider these questions.

- What area of the travel and tourism industry do I hope to work in?
- Is there a specific area of the industry that I would like to know more about?
- Are there specific skills that I would like to develop through work placement?
- What are the practicalities, such as transport, and the expected working hours?

Through group discussion, students should be encouraged to consider a wide range of options and evaluate their general effectiveness in terms of career and personal development. For example, a student hoping to eventually work in a travel agency might consider a work placement with a transport provider to gain experience and knowledge of a complementary area of the travel industry. A student who lacks confidence when dealing with customers in a face-to-face situation might choose a placement with any travel and tourism organisation that can provide training and regular exposure to customers.

Conduct during work placement

It is important that students understand the responsibilities that they have during work placements and the effect that poor conduct will have on the reputation of the college or school, its tutors, the course and themselves. This check list outlines what is expected of students during work placement.

Work placement conduct

- Find out the organisation's dress code before placement and make sure that you comply with it. Also understand regulations on issues such as make-up, hair, jewellery, etc.
- Identify and comply with any workplace rules and regulations. These might cover, for example, the use of telephones for personal use or areas where smoking is allowed.
- Ensure that you are always punctual and in the 'right place at the right time'. This includes coming back on time from meal breaks.
- If you are unable to get to work, contact the organisation and your tutor to let them know the reasons for, and expected length of, your absence.
- Discourage friends from visiting or contacting you at work as this is disruptive for the organisation.
- If you are unhappy with the placement for any reason, contact your tutor for advice and help. DO NOT simply walk out.
- Remember that customers will see you as a part of the organisation. Make sure that you make a good impression and are loyal to the organisation. Never criticise the organisation to customers or other staff.

- Remember that the work placement organisation is doing you a favour, not the other way round. Your presence creates extra work for staff, because they will be keen to ensure that you have a valuable placement. You need to be patient and tactful.
- At the completion of your placement, write a letter to the organisation thanking them for all the trouble that they have gone to in providing you with a placement. You might like to get your tutor to check your letter before you send it.

Formulating a work placement contract

One of the frequent criticisms of work placements is that students can feel that they are simply a dogsbody and don't gain any experience of value. Clearly, there are travel and tourism organisations that view placement students simply as free labour. However, the vast majority are keen to ensure that the placement is valuable.

One way to minimise the dogsbody problem is to encourage students to write and agree a work placement contract with the placement provider in advance. This does not need to be a complicated document but should simply set out the objectives of the placement and how they will be achieved. It is useful to include details of what the student will be doing during each day/week and how this will help them to meet their objectives. An example of a contract that might be used for a two-week work placement is on page 143 of this pack.

Collecting assessment evidence during work placement

There are a number of opportunities for students to collect assessment evidence during a work placement. You might like to provide students with a record sheet so that they can identify and record suitable information. (An example is given at the end of this pack, see page 144.) You can extend the record sheet to include assessment evidence for the optional units and key skills.

Using this form students might, for example, identify that they have opportunities to collect assessment evidence for unit 5, task 1: 'provide details of your dealings with at least five different types of customers in a variety of customer service situations and selling situations.' They might like to relate some of the evidence that they hope to collect to the objectives on their work placement contract. For example, objective one might be: 'to deal with a range of customers in a variety of different customer service and selling situations.'

Evaluating work placement

To ensure the value of work placement it is important that students evaluate their experiences after the placement. It is useful if they share their evaluation with the rest of the group, so that everyone can benefit from the issues raised. You might ask each student to prepare and give a short presentation to the group. Students can use information on the work placement contract and assessment evidence collected sheet as the basis for their evaluation.

Get students to start with a brief introduction to the work placement organisation, to cover travel and tourism sector, organisational structure, main products and services offered, target customers, etc. They should then outline:

- what they hoped to gain from the work placement
- what they actually gained
- the assessment evidence collected during placement
- conclusions.

Contacts and resource information

Most Vocational A level students will undertake a work placement with a local travel or tourism organisation. However, it is sometimes possible to contact national companies to identify any placement opportunities that they may have in your area. The websites listed on pages 461 to 464 of the textbook are a useful starting point.

Perhaps of more benefit, will be local contacts that tutors and students have. Organised visits also frequently provide students with opportunities to ask if organisations would be willing to offer a work placement.

Creating a work placement database

Once work placement is an established part of the course, it is extremely valuable to maintain a database of work placement providers as a reference for future groups of students. The database might be organised under these headings:

- organisation
- sector
- contact name
- telephone
- address
- e-mail
- types of placement offered
- past students undertaking placement (with dates).

Students can use the database to search quickly for suitable providers. For example, they could just print off work placement providers in the hospitality and catering sector if this is their preference. If your centre has an intranet, you might consider making the database available to students through this network.

Planning for work placement

1. Identifying the sector
What sector/s of the travel and tourism industry would I like to work in?

What other sectors are related to my chosen sector (that I would benefit from knowing about)?

How could I use the placement to collect evidence for my Vocational A level?

2. Identifying personal strengths and weaknesses
What am I good at?

Do I want a placement that will give me the opportunity to improve on my strengths and, if so, how?

What do I find difficult?

How could I use my placement to overcome some of my weaknesses?

3. Identifying placement providers
What are my constraints (for example, location, working hours, etc.)?

Which travel and tourism organisations might be able to provide a placement that would meet my needs?

4. Conclusion
What am I going to gain from my work placement?

Work Placement Contract

Student:	**Date of placement:**	**Work placement provider:**	**Work placement supervisor:**
Work placement objectives:			
1. 4.	2. 5.	3. 6.	
Overview of what the placement will include:			

How the work placement will cover the objectives. Write in what you will be doing each day and then tick the objective/s that you will cover.

	Activities	**Objectives 1**	**2**	**3**	**4**	**5**	**6**
Day 1							
Day 2							
Day 3							
Day 4							
Day 5							
Day 6							
Day 7							
Day 8							
Day 9							
Day 10							

Student's signature .... Tutor's signature.............................. Work placement supervisor's signature.................
Date Date Date

Assessment evidence collected during work placement

Unit 1 Investigating travel and tourism	
Assessment evidence	*Comments*
Unit 2 Tourism development	
Assessment evidence	*Comments*
Unit 3 Worldwide travel destinations	
Assessment evidence	*Comments*
Unit 4 Marketing in travel and tourism	
Assessment evidence	*Comments*
Unit 5 Customer service in travel and tourism	
Assessment evidence	*Comments*
Unit 6 Travel and tourism in action	
Assessment evidence	*Comments*